Knitter's Lib

Lena Maikon

Knitter's Lib

LEARN TO KNIT, CROCHET, AND FREE YOURSELF
FROM PATTERN DEPENDENCY

TEN SPEED PRESS
Berkeley | Toronto

A Penn Publishing Book
In association with

Ten Speed Press
Box 7123
Berkeley, California 94707
www.tenspeed.com

Distributed in Australia by Simon and Schuster Australia, in
Canada by Ten Speed Press Canada, in New Zealand by
Southern Publishers Group, in South Africa by Real Books,
and in the United Kingdom and Europe by Airlift Book
Company.

Edited by J. E. Sigler
Cover and text design by Catherine Jacobes Design

Library of Congress Cataloging-in-Publication Data
Maikon, Lena.
  Knitter's lib : learn to knit, crochet, and free yourself
from pattern dependency / Lena Maikon.
    p. cm.
  Includes index.
  ISBN-13: 978-1-58008-695-0
  ISBN-10: 1-58008-695-0
 1. Knitting. 2. Crocheting. 3. Knitting--Patterns. 4.
Crocheting--Patterns. I. Title.
  TT820.M25 2005
  746.43--dc22
                                        2005009472

Printed in Korea
First printing, 2005

1 2 3 4 5 6 7 8 9 10 — 09 08 07 06 05

Contents

Knit Blind No More

I grew up in a really big city, but it was surrounded by nothing for miles and miles, so getting knitting paraphernalia to our parts was a bit of a challenge. Although there were no yarn stores, every woman and girl on my block knew how to knit and crochet, had her collection of heirloom needles and hooks, and was an absolute pro at salvaging the yarn from store-bought or worn-out garments and stitching it into new ones. Naturally, when I turned 5, my grandmother started teaching me to knit. I was just entering upon the most exciting time in life, though, and was always busy with school or friends or sports, so I actually learned more about knitting by watching in amazement as my grandmother stitched away the hours than I did by knitting myself. In fact, in almost 25 years, I didn't knit anything but a cap and a pair of socks for my newborn baby brother.

In the meantime, I moved to a bustling, international city to study, eventually got my degree in mathematics, and started teaching. I was in a steady relationship, working 9 to 5, and I would have given my right hand to find a relaxing, silent, solitary hobby that could help me forget the lesson plans and "disciplinary actions" of the day. My boyfriend, seeing that I hated teaching and was generally frustrated by the drudgery in my life, one day brought home a handmade hat to cheer me up a little. I really liked it, but more importantly, it set off a little competitive spark in me when I realized that I could make it even better.

At least I thought I could. I had a degree in counting, at any rate, and my grandmother had given me a firm stitching foundation, so I bought a pair of needles and a few balls of cool yarn and started trying to outdo the anonymous hat knitter. I did, in the end, but the crucial point was that I had (re)discovered something I was passionate about, so I immediately tried to make the most of it. I stitched up a few more garments, carried them downtown to some expensive trendy stores, and asked the owners if they'd be interested in selling them. They were. I jumped on the opportunity, quit my miserable day job, stocked up on interesting yarns to inspire me,

was some sinister conspiracy to keep people knitting "blind" so that they'd keep buying patterns. I wouldn't fall for it. The majority of patterns were complex, form-fitting garments, and my style was urban, loosely comfortable, unisex clothes. So, rather than turn myself into a Victorian lady, I actually turned to the formulas I'd memorized in college and managed in the process to rediscover the long-lost logic behind knitting. Now, I am bequeathing these precious secrets to you, my fellow 21st-century knitters, as the 2 keys to independent garment design: *why* and *how*.

Formulas? Don't worry: there's nothing to memorize, I won't mention x- and y-variables, and we'll discuss Pythagoras's groundbreaking theory only twice (just kidding). Still, if you juice this book for all it's worth, you should come away with the understanding and ability to design and knit all the cool ideas you have for the "perfect" garment you could never figure out before. If you're attached to your store-bought patterns, you'll at least get advice: on how to make them fit perfectly every time, on when it's OK (and when it's not OK) to ignore "mistakes," and on how to simplify some majorly complicated needle operations. Even if you don't care about the why and how, you'll get some pretty cool streetwear out of this, right?

and had some labels printed with my new company's name, Leninka.

The only problem was that, when I was just getting started, I didn't always know how to knit every part of a garment. I occasionally looked for help in patterns, but I discovered that a lot of patterns took forever to knit, most of them demanded downright heroic stitching skills and experience, and no pattern ever explained to me *why* or *how*. (Have you ever understood why you knit shoulders the way you do?) At the peak of my frustration I imagined that there

WHAT YOU'LL FIND IN THIS BOOK...AND WHY	
easy-to-make, cool patterns that actually fit	because they're geometrically designed with simple shapes, not tightly knit along the wild contours of the (no-two-are-alike) human body
XL-size patterns	because big is beautiful, dammit
techniques that give you the sturdiest garment possible	because most of you probably live in cities infested with pigeons, construction, and crowded public transportation
the easy way to do traditionally hard stuff	if you *want* to ssk4tbltogskp2k8rib20p7CO 12dc3 with 4 needles when you could just inc 2 with a hook, by all means, go right ahead
some of the laws of mathematics	because you can't knit without them—and because they stipulate a few things that can't be knit; save yourself the frustration of trying to do the impossible and learn them up front
enlightenment	because it sucks to have to search 8 years for something sort of almost similar to what you have in your head— only to find out it doesn't fit quite right

WHAT YOU WON'T FIND IN THIS BOOK...AND WHY	
Queen Elizabeth apparel you need a girdle and a shoehorn to get into	because this is the 21st century, why else?
a D-cup bikini	because it's beyond the bounds of sanity and decency
knits so delicate you can't actually leave the safety of your home in them	because most of you probably live in cities infested with nightclubs, raves, and mosh pits
anything frustrating, complicated, or discombobulated	because the number of imaginable designs is infinite; don't waste time with hard ones
the actual laws of mathematics	because nobody understands them, so I just summed them up for you
instructions that give you a great sweater but no clue as to how you made it	because I take the time to explain it to you (I'm serious)

CHAPTER ONE

Basic Stitches (for Beginners)

Just in case you need it, here's an explanation for each of the basic stitches used in this book. If you've ever knit or crocheted anything before, you don't need this. If you're a beginner, though, start here and don't continue until you're comfortable making these stitches. If you need to feel like you're accomplishing something right away, it wouldn't hurt to make either of the scarves in this book to practice (most of) these stitches. (All instructions are for righties, by the way. If you're left-handed, you do the same, just with the hands reversed. I'm sure you're used to that.)

If you're practicing only to get familiar with the stitches (not with following a pattern or trying to make anything, that is), start with a 5 mm hook and 6 mm needles. If you feel they're too hard to work with, keep going up a millimeter until you get something comfortable. The yarn you practice with should be labeled suitable for whatever size hook or needles you're using, and it should be simple, not fancy or multistrand or with wacky tails flying off it. I teach my friends with Gedifra Fashion Trend and think it's a good practice yarn.

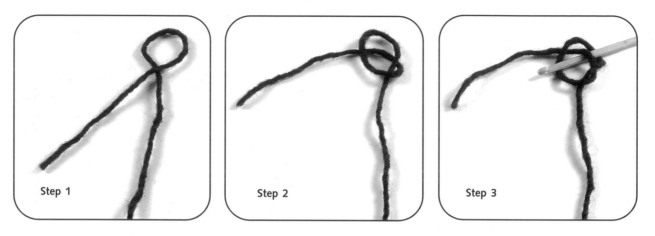

Step 1   Step 2   Step 3

General

"The Tail" versus "The Yarn"

Don't get confused by this. Fold the end of your ball of yarn over your finger. You've got 2 strands that hang down together: imagine them as completely separate pieces of yarn. The piece connected to the ball is "the yarn." The piece that ends in midair is "the tail." Yes, I know that the tail is still yarn and that it's also connected to the ball, but you need to ignore reality and remember what you just imagined in order to understand knitting and crocheting instructions.

Making a Slipknot

This gets yarn onto the hook or needle at the very beginning of any piece (or any practice).

1. Make a loop with the end of the yarn, leaving a bit of tail outside the loop (see step 1 above).

2. Bring the tail underneath the loop so that it looks like you're holding a NO [smoking, dogs, whatever] ALLOWED sign. (See step 2 above).

3. Insert your hook or needle down into the loop, underneath the bar of the NO . . . ALLOWED sign (see step 3 above), then pull up on that strand with the hook, making sure to hold tightly onto the tail and the yarn with the fingers of your left hand. You've got a loop on your hook/needle and a little knot below it, right? Good. That's a slipknot.

Crochet

(It comes first because it's easier.)

The Chain Stitch

Any and every crochet garment has to start with a row/round of chain stitches, so here's how to start from zero. First, remember this: when you're counting chain stitches, never count the slipknot at the beginning or the loop you have on the hook at the moment. They're not really chain stitches, so your instructions don't mean for you to count them.

1. If you don't have any yarn on the hook yet, make a slipknot to get some there.

2. Hold the hook in your right hand, so that the 2 strands of yarn hang down side by side. Insert your left index finger between the 2 strands, then clasp the tail between your thumb and middle finger, and gently pull the yarn taut. You should have something resembling a yarn triangle (see step 1 top right).

3. Make sure your left thumb and middle finger are close to the slipknot on your hook, then hook around the yarn (this is called "yarning over"—abbreviated yo; see step 2 bottom right), and pull it through the loop that's on the hook. (If you can't pull the yarn through the loop on the hook,

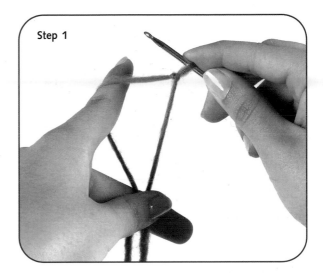

Step 1

Step 2

Making a Single Crochet

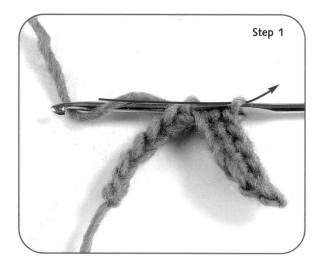

Step 1

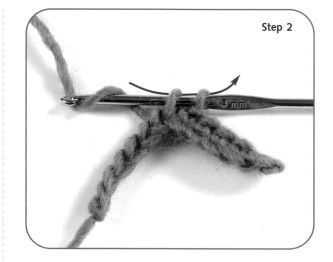

Step 2

you made the slipknot too tight. Just loosen it a little by gently tugging with the hook.)

4. From here, just continue yarning over and pulling the yarn through the loop on the hook. As you make more chain stitches, you'll get something that looks like . . . a chain. Make sure you keep your thumb and middle finger close to the stitch you just made; this really helps you control the movement.

Tightness and looseness are relevant (crucial, rather) to *everything* in knitting and crochet: holding yarn, making stitches, tying knots,

pulling tails, and more. It's really frustrating in the beginning to figure out what's too loose or too tight, but about all I can say is: practice lots, and you really will get a feel for it.

Single Crochet

You can't make this until you have a row of some other stitch, because you need a stitch to insert the hook into, so make a row of chains to practice on. When you're following a pattern, the instructions will always tell you which stitch to insert the hook through. For now, just make all your practice stitches in the chain stitch nearest to the hook.

Making a Double Crochet

1. Insert the hook through the stitch from front to back.

2. Yarn over (see photo on page 4, "Making a Single Crochet, Step 1"), and pull the yarn back through the stitch.

3. Yarn over again (see photo on page 4, "Making a Single Crochet, Step 2"), and pull the yarn through both of the loops on the hook.

Double Crochet

You can't make this stitch either until you've got a stitch to make it in, so make a chain or use the stitches you practiced before.

1. Yarn over, and insert the hook in the stitch from front to back (see step 1 above).

2. Yarn over, and pull the yarn back through the stitch. (You should have 3 loops on the hook right now.)

3. Yarn over (see step 2 above), and pull the yarn through the 1st 2 loops on the hook (those would be the last 2 you made).

4. Yarn over, and pull the yarn through the 2 remaining loops on the hook (see photo on page 4, "Making a Single Crochet, Step 2").

Making a Treble Crochet

Step 1

Step 2

Treble Crochet

You should notice now that a basic crochet stitch consists of yarning over twice and pulling the yarn through 2 loops on the hook. That basic stitch is the single crochet. To double it, what did you do? You yarned over 4 times and pulled twice through 2 loops on the hook. What do you think you'll do for a treble crochet?

1. Yarn over twice (see step 1 above), and insert the hook in the stitch from front to back.

2. Yarn over, and pull the yarn back through the stitch. (You should have 4 loops on the hook right now.)

3. Yarn over, and pull the yarn through the 1st 2 loops on the hook (the last 2 you made).

4. Yarn over, and pull the yarn through the next 2 loops on the hook (see step 2 above).

5. Yarn over, and pull the yarn through the remaining 2 loops on the hook.

Making a Double Treble Crochet

Making a Half Double Crochet

Double Treble and Treble Treble Crochet

Same thing as all the crochet stitches, except that, for a double treble, you yarn over 3 times in the beginning (see "Making a Double Treble Crochet" above), insert the hook through the stitch, then yarn over and pull through 2 loops repeatedly until you've got only 1 loop left. For a treble treble, yarn over 4 times in the beginning, then work as usual to get down to 1 loop. What's the difference between all these? Make a row of each and you'll realize right quick that it's the height of them.

Half Double Crochet

The half double crochet is the black sheep of the crochet stitch family. Make a few, and you'll see why.

1. Yarn over, and insert the hook in the stitch from front to back.

2. Yarn over, and pull the yarn back through the stitch. (You should have 3 loops on the hook right now.)

3. Yarn over (see "Making a Half Double Crochet" above), and pull the yarn through all 3 loops on the hook.

Making a Slip Stitch

Slip Stitch

Nuthin' simpler, but you probably won't be able to figure out what the heck it's good for without an explanation. For that, see page 56.

1. Insert the hook in the stitch.

2. Yarn over, and pull the yarn back through the stitch (see "Making a Slip Stitch" top left) *and* through the loop on your hook.

Joining New Yarn

This is a cinch.

1. Drop the old yarn; fold over the new yarn (leaving about 2" of tail), and lay it over your index finger just as you would for normal crocheting (see "Joining New Yarn in Crochet" bottom left).

2. Yarn over with the new yarn, and pull it through the loop on the hook (in other words, make a chain stitch).

3. Continue crocheting normally with the new yarn. After about 3 or 4 stitches, tie the tails of the old and the new yarn together, making sure to leave enough tail yarn to hide at the end of the project. (Too short a tail is not good for hiding: it'll just pop out of the hiding place. You want to be able to weave it in a good long way. See page 59.)

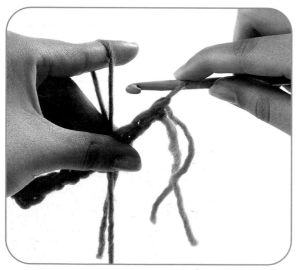

Joining New Yarn in Crochet

Knit

Casting On

What is it? It is to knitting what the base row of chain stitches is to crochet. In other words: the beginning. Before you do anything with the needle, though, fold over the end of your yarn with a tail at least 3 times as long as the width of your intended garment. (It won't be nearly that long by the time you're done, which is why it needs to be so long to start.)

1. Make a slipknot (see page 2) on the needle.

2. With your right hand, hold the needle horizontally so that both strands of the yarn hang down. Make sure your slipknot is underneath the needle, and that the tail end of the yarn is nearest your body.

3. Insert your left thumb and index finger between the 2 strands of yarn, grasp around both strands with your bottom 3 fingers, open wide your thumb and index finger (just the way you made a gun when you were 5), and twist your hand outward so that your palm is face up. The yarn should be wrapped around your thumb and index finger, with 4 strands crossing your hand (see step 1 top right).

4. With the index finger of your right hand (gently) holding down the slipknot on the needle, place the needle's point on your left wrist. Slide it up

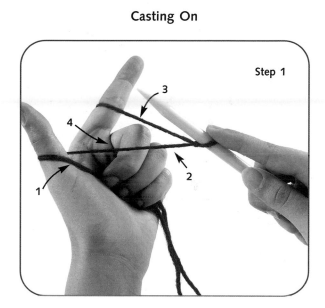

Step 1

Step 2

until you catch yarn (strand #1 in step 1 photo on page 9) on the needle, and make sure that strand #1 stays on top of the needle as you continue.

5. Place the needle's point on the tip of your left index finger above the strand of yarn there (strand #3), and slide the needle down toward your palm until you pick up strand #3. The 2 strands you've picked up should make an "X" over the top of your needle (see photo on page 9, "Casting On, Step 2").

6. Place the needle's point on the tip of your thumb, and slide it down your thumb between the strands on either side of your thumb. Pull your thumb out from between the strands, as you move the needle away from your hand to tighten the stitch; also catch the next strand #1 with your thumb and make a gun with your fingers again to tighten the knot of the stitch you just cast on.

Don't Forget

* Keep the knots you're making at the bottom of the needle straight and uniform (as much as possible, anyway, since this will take some practice). Stop now and then to even them and straighten them out with both hands.

* Don't pull the knots too tight on the needle, or you won't be able to continue knitting. How do you know if they're too tight? Grab the row of stitches by the knots at the bottom and try to slide them around on the needle. They should slide around very easily but keep their shape. (It's a rare knitter who casts on too loosely to knit, but, if you see space between the knots and the needle, then that's just what you've done.)

Knit Stitch

As I said, there are just 2 stitches in knitting, and once you've got them down, you can knit anything. Here's the first. (If you don't have a row of cast-on stitches on those needles, what in the world do you expect to practice with?)

1. Holding the yarn you're knitting with behind both needles, insert the right needle from right to left through the back leg of the loop on the end of the left needle (see photo on page 12, "Making a Knit Stitch").

2. Yarn over clockwise, pull the yarn back through the loop, and slide the loop off the left needle.

Alternate Knit Stitch

* **When:** The method you just used for making a knit stitch is great when you're knitting in stockinette stitch (see page 14), which you'll be doing most of the time. It's easy to stitch through the back leg of a stitch when that stitch sits like a post-purl loop, that is, to the right of the front leg (the way it does if it was purled on the previous row). Since stockinette stitch is made up of

How to Ride a Bucking Needle

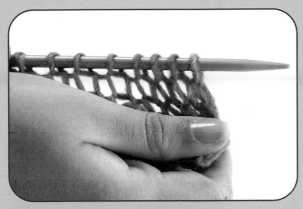

Post-Purl Loop

Post-Knit Loop

You can't do nuthin' with needles until you understand this: there are 2 parts to every knitted stitch. A stitch sits over your needle the way you would sit on a horse: with 1 leg on one side and 1 leg on the other. (If you catch a stitch riding sidesaddle, something's very wrong.) When you hold the needles in front of you to knit, 1 of those legs is going to be on your side of the needle. That's called the front leg (simply because it's closest to you, the knitter). The leg on the other side of the needle is the back leg.

Why is this important? Because there are 2 kinds of stitches in knitting, and there are 2 ways to make each of them. If you make a stitch the wrong way, you'll get a twisted stitch (or just a wrong stitch, or no stitch at all). Problem is, a lot of people can't tell a twisted stitch from a straight one, so look good and hard at the pictures here until you've got it down.

If you've just finished a row of purl stitches (and turned your work), your loops on the needle should look like this (see "Post-Purl Loop" above).

If you've just finished a row of knit stitches (and turned your work), your loops on the needle should look like this (see "Post-Knit Loop" above).

See how the post-purl loop has the front leg to the left of the back one? And the post-knit loop keeps the back leg to the left of the front one? That's the difference. If you see a knit stitch that rides like a purl, or a purl stitch mounted like a knit, it's because you twisted it.

How to fix it? Just slip that loop off the needle and immediately put it back on the way it's supposed to go; then knit it normally. Whenever you transfer a row from 1 set of needles to another, this is especially likely to happen, so really be on the lookout for it then. (It happens a lot to beginners, too.)

Making a Knit Stitch

Making an Alternate Knit Stitch

alternating rows of knit and purl, every time you need to knit you'll have a very convenient row of purled stitches to do it through. Sometimes, though, you don't knit in stockinette, and that's a problem. For example, when you knit in the round (which is knitting knit stitches all the time), or anytime you knit a knit row after another knit row, the legs of your stitches will look like post-knit loops, not post-purl loops (obviously).

* **How:** Instead of inserting your needle from right to left through the back leg of the loop, it's easier for most knitters to insert it from left to right through the front leg (see "Making an Alternate

Knit Stitch" above), which is exactly the same thing, even though it doesn't look like it. If it's not easier for you, do it the first way. To see exactly what happens and which you prefer, practice this a little on a swatch (a practice rectangle of knitted work; just start knitting, turn your work after every 15 or 20 stitches, and you'll have a swatch soon).

Purl Stitch

Stitch number 2 in knitting.

1. Hold the yarn you'll knit with in front of both needles, but with your finger behind the left

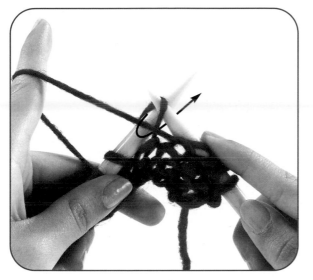

Making a Purl Stitch

Making an Alternate Purl Stitch

needle, such that the yarn hops over the top of the left needle. Insert the right needle from right to left through the front leg of the loop on the end of the left needle. (Make sure that the tip of the needle goes behind the yarn and then through the loop on the needle!)

2. Now move the yarn to the left of the right needle's point (see "Making a Purl Stitch" above), yarn over counter-clockwise, pull the yarn back through the loop, and slide the loop off the left needle.

Alternate Purl Stitch

* **When:** The 1st purl method, like the 1st knit method, is great when you're knitting in stockinette stitch (see below), because the post-knit loop from the row below always kicks that front leg forward for you to knit your purl stitches through. Whenever you knit a purl row after another purl row, though. . . .

* **How:** Insert the right needle from left to right through the back leg of the stitch instead (see "Making an Alternate Purl Stitch" above). Again, do it only if it really is easier for you than reaching the needle through the front leg. Of course, practice a little first, as always.

Binding Off Knit Stitches

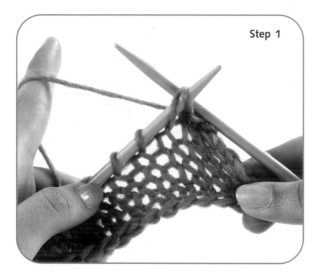

Step 1

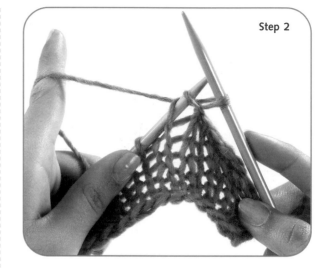

Step 2

Stockinette and Rib Stitch

You'll hear of these often. All the fancy stitch names in knitting really refer to just particular combinations of knit and purl stitches. These are the only 2 we'll use in this book, but there are lots more. Stockinette means to knit 1 whole row, then purl the whole next row, then knit the next, purl the following—you dig me. Rib means to knit 1 stitch, purl the next stitch, knit the next, purl, etc. Rib can actually be done in lots of combinations (knitting 2, or 3, or 4, or however many stitches, then purling the same number—or a different number—then knitting again), but we use only knit 1 purl 1 rib in this book.

Binding Off

There are 2 ways to bind off: knit and purl. (Naturally.) The only difference between them is where to hold the yarn (for a knit stitch or for a purl stitch) and which kind of stitches you're binding off (knits or purls). You already know those 2 things.

To Bind Off Knit Stitches

1. Hold the yarn behind your work, just as you do for a normal knit row. You basically are going to knit normally, but knit 2 stitches together each time where you would usually knit just 1.

Binding Off Purl Stitches

2. Insert the right needle through 1st 2 loops on the end of the left needle (see step 1 photo on page 14), yarn over, pull yarn through both loops (see step 2 photo on page 14), and drop both stitches completely off the left needle.

3. Make sure your yarn is still behind your work, then slide the loop on the right needle back onto the left needle, and start again from step 2 until you've got just one loop left on the right needle. Cut the yarn, and pull it through the last loop.

To Bind Off Purl Stitches

1. Hold the yarn in front of your work, just as you do for a normal purl row. You'll purl normally, but purling 2 stitches together instead of 1.

2. Insert the right needle through the 1st 2 loops on the end of the left needle (see "Binding Off Purl Stitches" left), yarn over, pull yarn through both loops, and drop both stitches completely off the left needle.

3. Make sure your yarn is still in front of your work, then slide the loop on the right needle back onto the left needle, and start again from step 2 until you've got just one loop left on the right needle. Cut the yarn, and pull it through the last loop.

Joining New Yarn

Also no sweat.

1. Drop the old yarn; fold the new yarn over your finger (leaving about 2" of tail), just as you would for normal knitting. Make sure to move it behind your work for knit and in front of your work for purl.

2. Insert the right needle through the stitch properly for a knit or purl stitch (whichever you're making; see photos on page 16, "Joining New Yarn in Purl" and "Joining New Yarn in Knit"), yarn over with the new yarn, and pull it back through the loop of

Joining New Yarn in Purl

the stitch (in other words, just make a normal stitch with the new yarn), and slide the stitch off the left needle.

3. Continue knitting normally with the new yarn. After about 3 or 4 stitches, tie the tails of the old and the new yarn together, making sure to leave enough yarn after the knot for you to hide at the end of the project. Remember that too short a tail is not good, and take into consideration any sewing you might need to do for the piece, because sewing with tails that were deliberately left extra long is usually a really good idea.

Joining New Yarn in Knit

CHAPTER TWO

Tips and Tricks to Perfect Your Knits

OK, here's where I explain how everything works. I didn't want this to be a totally boring review of the same old stuff you already know from every other knitting book, so I've tossed a couple of "tips and tricks to perfect your knits" into each section.

Since I began analyzing the knitting process, I've learned a lot of things most knitters I know either take for granted or never notice. Of course, I learned them the hard way, but that just inspired me to find easy ways to do hard stuff. No, it's not "cheating" (at least in my opinion). I figure, if it looks the same, it feels the same, and no one can tell the difference, why make it harder than it needs to be?

If you're a diehard traditionalist—or if for some reason you're convinced that self-affliction builds character—skip over the tricks; otherwise, I think you'll appreciate them. I hope that some will help you love (or at least feel neutral toward) whatever it is you've always hated or been really bad at doing.

Needles and Hooks

I always give metric measurements for needles and hooks, because I find it's the only system that makes sense. (I'm not alone.) The metric system is also just better: it has finer gradations (which mean more gauge options) and more accurate sizes. American needles are notoriously unreliable in terms of consistent measurements, because every manufacturer makes them differently.

Some brands show both American and metric measurement, and they're good if you use patterns from around the world. If you already have a stock of American needles, get a needle gauge (a little plastic or metal card with a bunch of holes in it). I wanted to give you a conversion chart, but I discovered that there are about a thousand versions and every manufacturer claims that its is the most accurate. "Yeah, right," I exclaimed, and decided to tell you just to get the needle gauge instead.

Swatches

Anyone who's ever knitted with a friend knows that the right-size needle and the right-size yarn aren't enough to give you the right gauge. Everyone knits differently—some tighter, some looser. For fitted garments, making a swatch is an absolute must. Since my patterns are mostly loose, comfortable clothes, though, it's not always crucial to follow a gauge. I deliberately selected designs that don't force you to "waste" a lot of stitches in preparation; you can build your wardrobe fast—and it'll fit both after the holidays and just before bikini season.

That's why I don't always provide the gauge for every type of stitch in a pattern. Where I don't, it means it doesn't matter (on crochet edging, for example). Where I do provide one, make a swatch, and adjust your needle size to get your gauge as close as possible to my gauge, but without obsessing over it. Really, it's not that important for most of these patterns.

Buying Yarn

Always buy extra yarn. A lot of things can happen in the course of a project, and you never know when you'll need it. (I once had to make one sleeve another color: when I went back to buy more yarn, the store had run out.) Even if you don't use it for that garment, a few balls of random yarn lying around can come in handy a few projects down the road. I even recommend that you use leftover yarn for some of the designs in this book.

Some yarns are like your little black dress—you just should always have them around: lightweight yarns in the predominant colors in your wardrobe are good for sewing on buttons; middle-weight yarns can be used to sew up accessories with visible seams; and heavy yarns can be turned into random fringes, appliqués, crochet linings, whatever. Don't (obviously) stock up on the $50-a-ball gold-frilled yarn, though: honestly, when would you ever use gold-frilled yarn again?

If your spare yarn pile gets out of control, stop and consider before you give some to the cat: thicker yarn gives cats a lot more to grab onto than lightweight yarn, so it's less entertaining—and makes for more vacuuming—for you. Sacrifice some of the lightweight stuff.

Substituting Yarn

I use only European yarns in this book, but I've checked that each one is readily available both online and in American yarn stores. (See page 170 for a list of my favorite online knitting suppliers; local yarn stores you'll have to call yourself—sorry, but America's real big and this book is real small.) If you still have trouble getting them, or if you prefer to use a different yarn, just remember the following principle of yarn substitution: same blend (more or less), same length per weight. Each company has some of the same basic blends, so that's not a problem. What I mean by "length per weight" is that 50 grams for a 100-yard ball of yarn is the same as 100 grams for a 200-yard ball (both numbers are doubled); 100 grams for a 100-yard ball is a shorter length per weight (half, in fact), so it's a heavier yarn.

You can use a yarn you're stuck on (or hold several strands of it together) and still follow a pattern that calls for something completely different, but you have to figure out which needles/hooks give you the same gauge. Once you get the same gauge, you can follow the pattern without any other adjustments and the final measurements will be the same, although the garment probably won't look and fall the same. In any case, think before you do something so drastic, and always make a swatch. Some yarns really aren't good for summer garments, but you can use just about any yarn you please for winter garments by holding 2 or 3 or however many strands together.

Reading Patterns

Always (always!) read my patterns all the way through before you start knitting. I often explain techniques or mention details of the design only after the written instructions. This isn't to make your life harder: if I put them earlier, you would probably get very frustrated (and confused) by the constant interruptions for explanations right in the middle of the directions.

If the pattern includes an element of design that you're unfamiliar with, find it in chapter 3, "Key Elements of Design," before you start knitting, and practice it. You might make it a few times and realize that, even though it looks super cool in the picture, you wouldn't want to be caught dead in it.

To get the most out of the design aspect of this book (or any pattern, for that matter), try to keep the big picture in mind as you knit. (I find that visualizing myself wearing the finished garment works best.) This puts the part you're working on in perspective, which improves your understanding of how the garment is built and why you're knitting the way you are.

Creating Clean Edges

If you're knitting a simple, 1-piece garment, such as a scarf or a shawl, you can create a cleaner edge on the garment by *not* knitting the 1st stitch at the beginning of each row; instead, simply pass the stitch off onto the right needle and begin knitting with the 2nd stitch. This goes both for knit and purl rows—indeed, for any type of stitch or pattern. (Exception: knit the 1st stitch in extended stitches no matter what. Edges should be strong, and extended stitches are rather delicate, not to mention impossible to sew or crochet through.)

If you're making a garment that you'll have to sew together, for instance, a sweater or pants, it's best to knit from the 1st stitch. If you were to pass it off onto the right needle, it would leave a hole too big to sew through. Some people prefer to pass off the 1st stitch all the time, and they just always sew pieces together through the 2nd stitch of each row, instead of between the 1st and 2nd stitches, as you'll do in this book.

Also, if you'll eventually crochet around the edges of a piece (to add a border or frills, for instance),

knit the 1st stitch. (Should you forget, though, or decide only later to add crocheting when the piece is done, make like the passionate passers and just crochet through the 2nd stitch.)

When you're knitting a garment with edges that need to be sewn as well as edges that won't, combine these 2 techniques to get the best edges all the way around: just knit the 1st stitches on edges that will be sewn, and pass off the 1st stitches on edges that don't need to be sewn. (Before you do, though, make sure you're clear about where all the pieces will go in the final garment—visualize, visualize, visualize.)

Stretching Your Work

You know how you stretch a finished garment just before you block it? Do the same thing at the end of every row (or as often as you can remember) to settle the yarn and put the stitches in their place. Frequent stretching reduces the number of awkwardly large-size and small-size holes in the final garment, and guarantees that you get enough yarn into the whole row for every stitch to have plenty of wiggle room. Sufficient yarn in the rows means that what usually pops, tears, or unties is less likely to do so. Always stretch only in the direction of the rows you're knitting (meaning from row to row, not side to side across a row).

Joining New Yarn

A Russian proverb says, "Measure 7 times before you cut." I don't think anybody actually does that, but you should at least remember that little piece of wisdom whenever you join new yarn. Here's my recommended method: pull the new yarn through the stitch of old yarn that's left on your needle or hook, drop the old yarn, knit or crochet a few stitches with the new yarn, and only then cut the old yarn.

What will happen if you do the opposite—that is, cut the old yarn and then join the new yarn in the next stitch of your work? The yarn that you cut is likely to slip back out of the 1st stitch or become so loose that it falls off the needle or hook—and that's 1 lost stitch. If you pay attention and leave the tail long enough, it's OK to cut the yarn before you knit the next few stitches. Most of us don't pay that much attention, though, and if you find your stitches keep mysteriously disappearing, definitely adopt my method.

No matter how or what you're knitting, it's good policy to join new yarn at the beginning of a row. If you're knitting something with lots of holes, it's not just good policy—it's practically Divine Law. You'll notice that a lot of my designs are pretty holey (full of holes, that is), and those holes just multiply the chances that your tails and knots will be seen while you're wearing the garment. So always make sure you have enough yarn to finish the next row *before* you begin it, and if you have even the slightest doubt, join the new yarn immediately. It will save you the frogging (or the social embarrassment) later. (This goes for crocheting, building on, adding on edging, and just about everything else.)

If you're going to be joining a lot of new yarn (as you do with stripes, for example), consider the "drop, twist, and add" method: When it comes time to switch to a new yarn, don't cut the old one; just leave it hanging off the garment and twist it once around the yarn you're knitting each time you pass it. When it's time to add the old yarn again, just pick it up and start knitting with it. It's not such a good method to use if you're going to knit with a single yarn for quite a stretch (I'd say more than 3 rows, and only 2 rows of extended stitches); in that case, just cut the yarn, and join it again later. But if you'll be switching back to that yarn in 3 rows or fewer, just pull it along, and save yourself the nuisance of joining again.

You can do this with a lot of my patterns, but I won't always explicitly tell you to do it. Learn these guidelines, read the pattern beforehand, and use your best judgment. You can usually tell by the picture whether a garment is a good candidate for this method (it is if it has a lot of different colors close together). One more tip: when you do pull yarn along, be careful not to pull it too tightly up the sides, otherwise it'll bunch up your rows.

Binding and Fastening Off

When you bind off the knitting patterns in this book, you might want to try a method that I find much easier and faster: use a crochet hook. This is my pet technique. People think I'm nuts, but I just love the hook. Try this at least once, if only for me. You might be shocked to discover a faster, easier way to bind off.

If you knit a piece with 6–10 mm needles, use a 5 mm crochet hook for binding off. If you knit with needles smaller than that, try a 2–3 mm hook. Really, though, whatever size hook gets your bind-off stitches the same size as your knit ones, that's what you should be using.

If you're binding off in knit, hold the yarn behind your work (just as you would to knit a stitch), insert the hook in the 1st stitch from front to back, pull the stitch off the needle, chain 1 with the yarn, *insert the hook in the next stitch on the needle, yarn over (see step 1 above), pull the yarn through the stitch on the needle and the stitch on the hook, and drop the stitch off the needle (see step 2 above); repeat from * until you have only 1 stitch left on the hook, then chain 1, and fasten off.

Binding Off Purl Stitches with Crochet Hook

Step 1

Step 2

If you're binding off in purl, hold the yarn in front of your work (hovering over the top of the needle, just as you would to purl), insert the hook in the 1st stitch on the needle from back to front, pull it off the needle, chain 1, *insert the hook in the next stitch on the needle (see step 1 above), pull the yarn through both stitches (see step 2 above), and drop the stitch off the needle; repeat from * until you have only 1 stitch left on the hook, then chain 1 and fasten off.

Nifty, eh?

"Fasten off" in crocheted patterns always means to chain 1 or slip stitch 1, cut the yarn, pull the end through to the back, and hide it. Whether you choose a chain or a slip stitch depends on what you're fastening off: use the slip stitch, which is less visible than a chain, on the front (or back) of a garment—anywhere you don't want it to be seen; use a chain on the back of a garment only, since it bumps up a little. If you don't mind the bump, a chain stitch does fasten the yarn down better than a slip stitch. When it's really important, I tell you which to use right before I tell you to "FO."

Finishing

I abhor sewing. I have traveled far and wide to learn as many techniques as possible to knit and crochet garments that require absolutely no sewing up, and when none of the super-grandma-knitters could give me any, I still "sewed" with my crochet hook.

That's why, in almost all my patterns, I recommend that you use a 2 or 3 mm crochet hook to hide yarn ends. It's why nearly all the pieces you'll "sew" together are done either with slip or single crochet stitches. And it's why all the instructions for lining, edging, fringing, and that other fancy stuff assume that you're using a hook, not a stupid needle. Unfortunately, there really is no way to sew on buttons other than with a needle, but you'll find that silver sliver very rarely employed here.

If you're not so familiar with the blessings a crochet hook can bestow, try following my (yes, detailed) instructions instead of just doing stuff the way you already know. I find that using a hook lets me work 10 times faster and 100 times easier; plus the possibilities it opens up are infinitely more interesting than anything you can do with those sharp pointy things.

Creating "Sewn Seams" with Crochet

A lot of people don't know how to use a crochet hook to sew, so I'm going to give you a brief intro. For a person as averse to sewing as I am, crocheting is the only thing that keeps me from walking around with my knits taped together. But there's a plus for you needle-lovers, too: external seams made with lovely single, double, half double, and all the other types of crochet stitches. (Yeah, I know, you can do neat stuff with a needle, too. I'm not interested.)

There is, however, one time you shouldn't sew with a hook, and that's when you need to make a really smooth, thin, almost invisible joint between 2 pieces, such as for very delicate-looking garments. For that, sewing with a needle and thread (or very thin yarn) really is best. Because you crochet pieces together with yarn, and yarn is thicker than thread, and because crocheting just makes knottier stitches than real sewing, crocheted seams are more visible than needle-sewn ones. Even if you try to hide them, crocheted seams might bulge a bit when you strike a certain pose. Since most of the patterns I give you are streetwear, not delicate-looking stuff, you'll do almost all sewing with a hook and take full advantage of it by making visible seams that add to the designs.

There are 2 ways to sew anything: visibly or invisibly. When you're sewing in crochet, use slip stitches to create a more invisible stitch, and use single or half double crochets for visible seams.

Here's the gist of it: Pull your 2 pieces together, line up their edge stitches, and (I recommend, at least) place safety or straight pins in a few of the stitches near the edge to keep them properly lined up. Insert the crochet hook in the corner stitch of the 1st piece, through the same stitch in the 2nd piece,

Sewing with Slip Stitches

Sewing with Single Crochet Stitches

and chain 1 (or slip stitch 1, if you're going for less visibility), then just make 1 stitch (slip, single, or half double crochet) in each pair of stitches all along the edge of the 2 pieces. (See photos above.) Try to stitch between the 1st and 2nd stitches of each row, but if you don't have holes there, just put the stitching in the 2nd stitch. At the end, chain 1 (or slip stitch 1), and fasten off.

Blocking and All That Fun Stuff

I don't actually block my stuff. You can if you want, but it's necessary for only a few garments in this book, and I tell you which ones at the end of those patterns. Even those, you don't really block: you just iron them (or part of them) to even out the stitches.

The most important thing to remember about blocking, ironing, and washing your knits is to read the manufacturer's instructions. Every yarn is different (really different these days), so go with what the yarn label says no matter what any pattern promises will work. (One exception: despite a manufacturer's claims, I never put my knits in the washing machine. If you really want to try, first throw in a swatch—knit with the yarn you want to wash, obviously—and see how it comes out before you place a week's work in the same precarious position.) The second most important thing to remember is *never* to rub an iron along your knits. Just rest it on one spot, pick it straight up in the air, rest it on the next, pick it up again . . . you get the drift.

Most of you probably already know this stuff, but just in case you need to refresh your memory, when I tell you that a garment needs blocking, here are general guidelines: Always turn your garment wrong side out, place a slightly damp (clean!) cloth towel on top, turn your iron to medium heat (lowest heat possible for wool or wool blends), and iron lengthwise (that is, with the iron length extending from row to row), not side to side (from stitch to stitch along a row). If it's a multiple-piece garment that you had to sew together, stretch the seams lengthwise a bit as you iron. And keep that towel damp by spraying it with water whenever it starts to get a little parched—otherwise you're likely to singe right through it and your precious knit.

CHAPTER THREE

Key Elements of Design

Welcome to the nucleus of this book—and of the fashion world. As you make your way through each project that follows, you should constantly refer back to this section not only to learn any technique you're unfamiliar with but also to understand all the elements of design featured in the garment you're knitting.

I admit it: this list is not exhaustive. But how could it be? The most basic elements of design are simply a result of the laws of mathematics, but the more complex ones are highly flexible and therefore subject to the whims and fancies of every individual knitter. (Sometimes, despite thousands of years of knitting history, some lucky lady even manages to come up with a totally new one.) Shorten them, lengthen them, toss them all together, add a nice dressing . . . that's the whole meaning of the word "design." Everyone can do it.

Here I've put together some of the simplest, most common elements to get you started. With a bit of practice, you'll understand them in no time, and then every other design you'll ever see will be at your creative mercy.

Knitting versus Crocheting

In the modern world of handmade garments, crocheting has become something like the ugly little sister of knitting and sewing, not as appreciated these days as she should be. She can, after all, spruce up your knits impressively: you'll soon see that 1 hook can pull off a lot of things 2 needles could never dream of.

I know a lot of kick-ass knitters who are just plain afraid of crocheting. As you'll see, though, it has a lot to offer in both garment design and understanding the science behind it.

Precisely because you knit with 2 needles, knitted pieces are always flat. So any garment that the outrageously unflat human body can slip into has to be knit in several flat pieces and then sewn together. You could also knit those pieces in the round or with 4 needles, but all that does for you in the end is make you sew a little less. With crocheting, however, the single hook has (almost) unlimited freedom of movement, which, for you, means the freedom to stitch a practically infinite variety of patterns, shapes, and even 3D thingamajigs such as flowers, animal faces, cat and baby toys, whatever.

Crocheting is more convenient for summer garments, because you can stitch a lighter, more open (hence ventilated) piece. Knowing how to crochet opens up the possibility to add it on the edges of knit pieces, or to spruce them up with other add-ons. It also means that you have more options for sewing: invisibly or visibly with beautiful, decorative stitches. (It's faster than sewing with a needle, too.) Basically, learning to crochet just broadens your horizons and gives you more options for making all your handmade knits more attractive and closer to exactly what you imagined.

I don't use any really complicated stitches in this book, but if my explanations in chapter 1 didn't help you (these things are very individual, you know), you should remember that the best, fastest, cheapest way to learn new stitches is from the back of a crochet magazine. Just flip through a few at the store until you find one of those 2-page spreads that gives instructions and pictures for a whole bunch of crochet stitches. Most magazines have those pages, and you can learn tons from them for less than $5.

How Every Single Garment Is Built: Height and Width

Every stitch you knit or crochet performs a function in the larger picture that is the garment. It builds height or width, connects other stitches, increases, decreases, knots things closed, or the like. Theoretically speaking, this works pretty much the same in knit and crochet. But practically speaking, there is a huge difference, and you can learn a lot more about how garments are built by studying the stitches in crochet. Let me give you a basic introduction, and you'll soon see why.

The Fundamental Difference between Knit and Crochet

Knitting (on 2 needles) is flat, while crochet is 3-dimensional. If you think that doesn't make a big difference, imagine the way a wall-ramming ferret must see things compared to the way you see them. Because you knit in just 2 dimensions, you work in 1 direction all the time, along either the length or the width. There's nothing to be done about this because you knit with 2 needles, which means that everything is stuck between them. The knitting binds the needles to each other and restricts their movement, so, to change to another plane in knitting, you have to bind off, and then go back, pick up stitches, build on, and so on.

Crochet uses just 1 hook that is connected to the yarn only, so you can swing it around any way you want and switch to another plane at any moment. All you have to do is insert the hook in a new stitch and start stitching in a new direction. The next stitch will hold the yarn in the new plane.

Height and Width of Stitches

In knitting, the height and width of all stitches you make with the same yarn on the same needles is uniform (ideally, at least). That simple fact doesn't give me much of an opportunity to clarify the science of stitching, though, so let's move right on to crocheting.

All crocheted stitches that you make with the same size hook and the same yarn have the same width. Put into a formula, the width of:

1 chain=1 single crochet=1 half double crochet= 1 double crochet=1 treble crochet, and so on.

The height, though, varies considerably with the stitch. A row of crocheting is always made up of at least 2 types of stitches—chains and crochets—so it's seriously important to know how to match chains to the various heights of crochet stitches. You don't want the beginning of a row $1/2"$ taller than the rest of the row, after all. Once you know the correlation, you can write your own perfectly mathematically sound patterns without even picking up a hook, and the stitches will match perfectly, too.

The basic stitch in crocheting is the chain stitch, and there's no stitch shorter than that. The chain is also the stitch that starts every row and round in crocheting, so it's the standard by which you measure all other stitches.

Have a look at the table that follows, refer back to it as you crochet, and you'll soon understand why you crochet every stitch you do and what function it performs. Believe it or not, that little bit of knowledge can set you free from pattern dependency and provide all you need to design your own garments.

STITCH EQUIVALENCIES TABLE

the height of	equals the height of
1 chain	1 single crochet
1–2* chains	1 half double crochet
2 chains	1 double crochet
3–4* chains	1 treble crochet

*Depends on how tightly or loosely you crochet.

Beginning and Ending Rows

In knitting, height and width are built practically automatically with each knit or purl stitch. Usually you flip your work to begin a new row, and you either knit or purl or do a pattern of the 2 kinds of stitches across, creating a row the height of those uniform stitches.

If you're knitting in the round, you connect the last cast-on stitch to the 1st stitch of the 1st row you'll knit, joining them into a circle. Before you join them, check carefully that your stitches aren't twisted around your needle; you want the knots of all the cast-on stitches at the bottom of the needle. After that, the last stitch of each round is followed by the first stitch of the following round.

Building Height with Chain Stitches at Beginning of a Row

In crocheting, rows or rounds always begin with chain stitches. Why? Chains are the only stitches that bring your hook to the top of the next row or round. Try starting a row with any other stitch, and you'll quickly see that your hook is scrunched down at the previous row, unable to build up height for the next row. Of course, the number of chains you'll use has to equal in height the stitch you'll build the rest of the row with, as you see in the example of double crochet (see photo above).

Ending a row in crocheting is a bit trickier. You want your edges to be uniform, so for each pattern you have to figure out which stitch will give you a straight edge. Obviously, if chains build up height, they're not going to come in very handy for fastening down the end of a row, and that's why you never see

Finishing a Row with Double Crochet

Row Finished with Double Crochet

them performing that function. In this book, an edge stitch will always be the same as the tallest stitch that appeared in the pattern used on that row. Whatever stitch (other than chain) you choose to use in your own patterns, it's important to make the last stitch of a row through the highest stitch at the end of the previous row. (See photos above.)

For ending rounds in crochet, the slip stitch is the star. It has the wondrous capability of connecting 2 stitches together without building any (noticeable) width or height between them, so rows are connected by simply slip stitching 1 through the highest chain you made at the beginning of the row, which connects it into a round (see photos on page 32, "Connecting Chains into a Round" and "Connecting Double Crochet Stitches into a Round").

Putting It All into Practice

Whichever patterns you pick to knit or crochet in this book, you'll notice a big difference between the way they're written from what you're probably used to: I don't give you just a big block of instructions, but rather I break things up step by step. What a lot of undiscerning knitters and crocheters get out of that big block is just a big block of a garment. I aim to make you stop and pay attention to how a garment is built, let you see the elements of each garment, each piece, each row, and each technique.

You'll probably get used to this "interruptive" style after reading a pattern or two, and I hope you'll achieve this goal: that you'll get dozens of garments out of every single pattern in this book—or at least dozens of ideas and the understanding to make

Connecting Chains into a Round

Connecting Double Crochet Stitches into a Round

them. And, if you didn't understand a word of the abstract mumbo jumbo you just read, don't worry: mark this page, skip to a pattern, and, the second you recognize something from here, flip back and read it again. You'll get it, I guarantee.

Crochet Techniques

Under versus In/Through

My designs are simple only in the sense that they're not hard to make. They probably use a few elements of design that you haven't run across in other patterns before. Most things that might be new to you I'll explain the moment I tell you to do them, but there is one really important thing that applies to just about every pattern in this book: crocheting under a stitch

is *not* the same as crocheting in or through a stitch. You probably already know this from knitting, where it's really obvious. There's a huge difference in crochet, too, and it's a distinction you've got to be able to make if you want your own pieces to measure up right and to come out looking the way you expected.

What difference does it make? A really big one: Crocheting under a stitch places the next row right on top of it (in the same plane). Crocheting through a stitch makes the row you're working on kind of lean back (or forward, depending on which leg of the stitch you crochet through) on the previous row.

What's the difference in the stitch itself? Well, it depends on the stitch. First, it's impossible to crochet under a chain stitch. You simply have to stitch through the 2 little legs that form it. For a slip stitch, however, "through" means to insert the hook between the 2 little legs that form the stitch, while "under" means to insert the hook below *both* of them. You can see how the latter case would build the next row directly on top of the stitch, and how there's no way it could lean back or forward from it; the former, on the other hand, attaches the next row beside the upper half the stitch, so it's going to stick out a bit.

The anatomy of single crochet and all taller stitches makes them special. Stitch up a few single and double crochets, and then come back to this page. See how the stitch has 2 components: a column topped by a chain stitch? The chain stitch, which sits flat atop the stitch, is the key here. Though it is possible to stitch through it, you never will. Always stitch under that little chain on top, so that you build up from between it and the column. Here's the confusing part: this is called stitching through (or in) a single, double, treble, whatever crochet stitch. It is, technically, since you're getting in between the 2 parts of the stitch, even if you are thinking to yourself "under the chain."

As for knit stitches, you can't possibly stitch under them. You'll always stitch through them, or between 2 separate stitches. The difference is obvious, though, and you've probably done it a million times by now, so I'm not going to go into the gory details.

Turning Corners

Just about any time you crochet a border onto an edge that isn't round, you're going to have to turn corners, and there's a science to doing it. Try to imagine it on, say, a triangular bikini cup ('cuz I've got one in this book): if you make 1 stitch in the last stitch on side A of the triangle, just 1 stitch in the corner, and continue over to stitch 1 in the 1st stitch of side B, you'll be stretching your yarn mercilessly around that corner. The stretched yarn will bunch up the corner of your garment, and that's not only ugly but also uncomfortable.

So here's what you have to do: make the last stitch in side A, stitch a few times in the corner stitch to fill it up and slowly inch your way over to side B (see photo below), and then continue crocheting as

Turning Corners in Single Crochet

usual along side B. This reinforces your corner and holds it nicely in place. You can turn corners with stitches in pattern, as well, such as fans or windows, but you'll see that when you do corners in patterns, you use only 1 pattern group right on the corner. That's because each fan or window is made up of more than 1 stitch already, so you get multiple stitches in the corner even with a single fan or window.

The angle of the corner makes a difference: you might need to make 3 stitches in a 60° angle but 5 in a 30° angle. You can also break up this "inching around" by not stitching 3 (or whatever) in the corner but instead stitching 2 in the next-to-last stitch on side A, 2 in the corner, and 2 in the 1st stitch on side B. Just make sure you create a smooth curve that doesn't stretch your yarn. If your corner looks a little funny, try it with more stitches, try it with fewer, and recognize that not having the right number is most likely the problem.

In this book, you'll need this little bit of info mostly for finishing garments with crocheted edging, but it is relevant to every corner you'll ever turn with a crochet hook.

Net

Net is majorly useful for all sorts of summer wear. It also can be used to make a classy-looking outer garment that you can wear over warmer stuff in the winter. I wear net garments mostly over my plain clothes to dress myself up a little for special occasions, but it's sturdy enough to wear even on the street. Once you understand the (simple) logic behind it, you'll be able to design your own garments by playing with the sizes of the rectangles.

A net pattern is made up of rectangles, which are made up of 2 vertical sides and 2 horizontal sides. The height is formed by the vertical columns on either side of the rectangle, and the width is formed by the horizontal rows that form the rectangle's top and bottom. The height of a rectangle in net can be built up with any type of crochet stitch, from as short as a single crochet to as long as a treble treble crochet (or even more). The width can be as long as you want, too, but it is built only with chain stitches, of which you need at least 1 (obviously) to separate the rectangle's sides. I promise that all this will actually make sense to you once you've read the rest of this section and tried to crochet a few rows of net.

After you've got a base row of chains from which to build the garment, you crochet the 1st row or round of rectangles. The 1st rectangle always begins with chain stitches (which, as I said earlier, build the height of a row or round in crochet), and you should decide how many you need to make by using the Stitch Equivalencies Table on page 30. To give you an example, though: if you want the columns of the rectangles to be 1 single crochet, you'd make only 1 chain stitch at the beginning, since 1 chain is the height of a single crochet and will make your 1st column equal to your 2nd; if you want the columns to be made of treble crochets, you'd make 3 chain stitches at the beginning.

Next, you make chains for the width of your 1st rectangle; let's say it will be 4 chains wide. Then, it's very important where you insert the hook for the 2nd column in the rectangle; if your rectangles will be 4 chain stitches wide, you need to insert the hook in the 5th chain from the chain stitch in which you began the 1st column (see photo below). Think about it: 1 column in the 1st stitch, 4 chains for width match chains 2–5 at the bottom, and the 6th stitch (5 stitches from stitch 1) is where your 2nd column should be made.

On later rows it will be obvious where you should insert your hook. But there are 2 different places for

Spacing First Row of Rectangles in Net

later rows, because there are 2 kinds of net: "staggered" net, in which the columns that form the sides of the rectangles don't line up, and "parallel" net, in which the columns do line up.

Staggered Net

For staggered net, you need to begin every row after the 1st by slip stitching 1 through each of the chains that form the width of the 1st rectangle on the previous row until you reach its center. This places the 1st column of the 1st rectangle on the new row in the middle of the 1st rectangle on the previous row. (That's the whole "staggered" thing.) Once you've got your hook in the right stitch, you chain up to make the 1st column of the row (see photo on page 36, "Beginning New Row in Staggered Net"), you chain across to make the width, and then you insert the hook under the center (not through the center stitch) of the next rectangle on the previous row.

Keep making your rectangles to the end, but at the end, you insert the hook through the middle stitch of the last rectangle in the previous row (yes, through the stitch, which fastens it tighter than just wrapping it around; see photo on page 36, "Ending Row in Staggered Net"). Stopping at the center of the last rectangle gives you consistent edges on either end of the row.

This schema obviously will not give you a square piece. Imagine it and you'll see that you've got half a rectangle missing on either side of every row, so the staggering automatically decreases the width of the

Beginning New Row in Staggered Net

Ending Row in Staggered Net

piece in a triangular fashion, like a shawl. If you connect the 2 ends of every row, it also works wonderfully for circular pieces. (How to connect the ends? When you get to the end of a row, just make however many chains you need for the width of the last rectangle, then slip stitch through the last chain you made for height at the beginning of the row.) If you want to use staggered net in a square piece, however, you have to make half a rectangle on each end instead of slip stitching your way to the center of the 1st rectangle and stopping in the center of the last one.

The really cool thing about staggered net is that it actually looks like hexagons when it hangs down, because the weight of the garment pulls the bases of

the rectangles into diagonal-looking lines between the columns. This is an effect you can't get with parallel net, because the columns line up, so they carry one another's weight instead of pulling on the bases.

Parallel Net

Parallel net is much easier to explain (but both of them are simple once you have a hook in your hands): just make your base row of chains, your 1st row of rectangles, and on every consecutive row, make the vertical columns of the rectangles in the exact same stitch that forms the side of the rectangle on the previous row. This makes a very nice square garment (see photo on page 37, "Making Parallel Net"), or a round one if you join the edges (at the end of a row, just slip

Making Parallel Net

stitch through the last chain that builds the height of the 1st rectangle at the beginning of the row).

To make a triangle with parallel net, you slip stitch in at the beginning of each row, just as you would for staggered net, except that you go all the way to the 2nd column, so that your rectangles still line up; at the end of a row you obviously stop 1 whole rectangle short of the edge.

Increasing and Decreasing in Net

The key to increasing and decreasing in net, for both staggered and parallel, is to keep making the vertical columns in the same stitch on the previous row— as if you weren't increasing or decreasing anything. If you don't do this, you'll notice real quick how parallel rectangles are no longer parallel, and staggered rectangles look like they were staggered by a 3-year-old. Even when increasing and decreasing, always line up the sides of the rectangles in parallel net, and start rectangles at the center of those on the previous row in staggered net, just as if you weren't making any changes. Also, never increase height or width *within* a single row—God only knows what you'll wind up with if you do. All the rectangles on a row should be the same height and width; increase and decrease only for the entire row.

To increase the height of rectangles in net, just increase the number of chains at the beginning of the row, and then use the crochet stitch with the corresponding height for all the other vertical columns on that row. To decrease, decrease the chains and match the crochet stitch. For instance, if your row starts with 2 chains, and the rectangles' columns are half double crochets, when you want the next row to be twice as high, you start with 4 chains and make all the rectangles' columns with treble crochets.

To increase or decrease the width of rectangles in net, just increase or decrease the number of chains that form the width of the rectangles. Everything else stays the same.

Windows

Windows, as I call them, are like tiny little net patterns, usually added to the edge of an otherwise finished garment. They're smaller and more delicate

Making Windows

than the big rectangles I use to crochet an entire garment in net, and they're really convenient (even necessary, in my opinion) for weaving extra stuff through at the end, such as straps or ties that hold something on or keep something closed. You'll use them a lot, so read the logic behind the net pattern (see pages 34–37) and know that a window is basically the same: a small crochet stitch (usually a half double crochet) attached to another stitch—but also separated from it, which is what creates the hole or "window"—by a chain stitch or two (see photo above).

Shells

Shells are several stitches made through a single stitch in the previous row, a technique commonly called a "cluster" in crochet patterns. They're great for making triangular and round pieces without headache, and they make pretty nice rectangular pieces as well, with a little planning.

The height of a shell can be formed by a double crochet or any taller stitch. The width depends on the number of stitches you make through the same stitch on the previous row. In other words, if I create a shell that has 4 treble crochets going through a single stitch on the previous row, its height is equivalent to 3 chains (see the table on page 30) and its width is equivalent to 4 chains.

The 1st row of shells, like the 1st of net, is a little harder than the rest, because you have to consider and space for width. Have a look at the photo on page 39, "Spacing First Row of Shells". See how, between two shells, the space above the stitches on the previous row is filled by *both* shells? Because the shells fan to the sides, half of 1 shell fills up half the space, and the other half of the space is filled up by the adjacent side of the other shell.

With that in mind, whenever you start a row of shells, you first build for height by making chain stitches—whichever number is equal to the height of the stitch you'll make your shells from. (Since a shell has to be at least a double crochet tall, you'll need at least 3 chains at the beginning of each shell row. See the Stitch Equivalencies Table on page 30.)

What you do next depends upon whether you want a triangular, a square, or a round piece. For a triangular piece, the next step is to insert the hook in the stitch that is half the width of 1 of your shell patterns. Why half? The 1st shell is on the edge of the garment, so there's no shell sitting beside it to take up the other half of that space. Only half of the 1st shell fans out toward the edge, so you need to put only half the shell's space between it and the edge. In other words, if my shells are all 4 stitches wide, I'll need to insert my hook in the 3rd stitch from the edge, leaving a 2-stitch space for the right-hand half of the shell to fill.

For a square piece, you insert the hook in the same stitch that your chains originated in, and you make a half shell to create a clean edge. For a round piece, you insert the hook in the same stitch that your chains originated in and make a whole shell. Even if you have a clearly triangular, square, or round piece, though, every garment is different, so look closely at your edges and play around with them a little until you get just the design you want. I'm giving you general guidelines, and it's best if you experiment with them a little.

Along the rest of the 1st row, you place the same number of stitches between shells as each shell is wide. For our hypothetical shell 4 stitches wide, this means that after you've done the 1st shell, you'll make the next shell in the 5th stitch—not the 4th — from the hook. You don't make it in the 4th because that would leave only 3 stitches between the shells,

Spacing First Row of Shells

and that's not enough to accommodate their width. (See photo above.)

You can, actually, not accommodate the width of shells deliberately in order to make them look more frilly. By inserting the hook in a closer stitch, you reduce the amount of space they have to fan out, which forces the sides of the 2 shells to bunch up together, creating a frill. (Because you then put more shells on a row in order to fill it up, this is also a way to increase.)

On all consecutive rows, you've got 2 options: "staggered shells," which are placed in the space between the shells on the previous row, and "parallel shells," which are each placed right on the center of the shell below on the previous row.

Making Staggered Shells

Making Parallel Shells

Staggered Shells

A staggered-shell pattern generally has a chain stitch or two between shells. Those chains make a very convenient seat for the shells that will come on the next row (see photo above): you can easily see exactly where the stitches between 2 shells are, and easily build the next row's shell by inserting your hook under them. Since all staggered shells sit between the shells from the row below, putting a few stitches between shells helps you get perfect, even staggering all the way around.

If you use a staggered-shell pattern in a square garment, on the 2nd and all even-numbered rows of shells you make a half shell at the beginning of the row, then chain as usual, insert your hook under the chains that connect the next 2 shells on the previous

row, continue making shells all the way across, and end with another half shell on the other end. To stagger shells in a triangular garment, slip stitch at the beginning of the row to climb up to the point between the 1st 2 shells on the previous row, then chain for height and width, insert your hook between the next 2 shells of the previous row, and make whole shells all the way to the end. You'll notice that staggered shells in a triangular garment automatically decrease the piece by half a shell on either side.

Parallel Shells

A parallel-shell pattern typically creates chains between the sides of the shells themselves, for the same reason that you put them between whole shells in the staggered shell pattern: they give you a nice convenient spot to attach the next row of shells. The chains between the 2 sides of a shell wind up looking like a little center arch connecting the sides (see photo on page 40, "Making Parallel Shells"), which is pretty cute in addition to being convenient.

To create rows of parallel shells, you make the shells of one row right on the centers of the shells on the previous row. Start the 2nd and all consecutive rows of shells by first chaining up the number of chain stitches equal to the height of your shells. (For rounds, start a new round by first slip stitching up to the center of the 1st shell on the previous round, then chain for height.) Next, insert your hook under the chains in the center of the 1st shell on the previous row, and make the 1st shell of the new row. Continue to make shells under the center chain stitches the same way to the end.

Chains and Endings in Shells

Staggered shells usually look better without chains between the 2 sides of a single shell, and parallel shells often look better without chains between shells. If you're designing your own garment in either shell pattern, the chains I recommend aren't actually necessary. (In my patterns, though, they absolutely are.) If you don't like them or they don't serve your purposes, just don't make them. Or add more, if you choose: put chains both between shells and between the sides of a shell in a staggered shell pattern or in a parallel shell pattern. (Adding more than 1 chain between the 2 sides of a shell isn't a good idea. It tends to make the shells look like they're breaking open. There's definitely a maximum here.) Whatever you decide to do, the key to good design is to be consistent across the row. You can change between rows, but multiple shell designs on a single row just look busy.

Now, if you were paying really close attention, you probably asked yourself this question: Doesn't putting chains between the 2 sides of a shell increase the width of the shell? No. Remember my definition earlier: the width of a shell depends on the number of stitches originating in a single stitch on the previous row. Chains that come between these stitches don't originate there. They're made at the top of the column and just kind of hover over the stitch on the previous row. So even if a shell has 2 double crochets on 1 side, 2 chains in between, and 2 double crochets on the other side, the width of the shell is still only 4 double crochets, and you should place only 4 stitches between shells when you're spacing them on the 1st row.

Increasing in a shell pattern is usually done either by increasing the number of chain stitches *between whole shells* or by increasing the number of crochet stitches that make up the shells themselves. The 1st technique increases the space between the shells, and the 2nd makes the shells themselves wider. Decreasing, of course, works just the other way around: you make fewer chains between shells or fewer crochet stitches in a shell.

Connecting Shells into a Round

Fan Border

How to end? A round of shells is ended the same as any other crochet round: with a slip stitch through the highest chain at the beginning of the round to connect the 2 ends into a circle (see photo above). A row of shells is ended with a half shell or a whole shell, whichever you began the row with.

Fans

Just as windows are basically a net pattern for adding to edges, fans are basically shortened shells to add on as frills (see photo above right). Since shells can be made only with a double crochet or any taller stitch, fans are made up of a single crochet on 1 side, 2 chains (separators), and a half double crochet on the other side—all short compared to the shell. You can add extra chains between fans, just as you can between shells, to space them out more.

They're made just the way shells are, as a "cluster" originating from a single stitch in the previous row (or along an edge). To start a row, round, or edging of fans, chain 3 and half double crochet 1 in the same stitch. Then *single crochet 1 in the 2nd stitch from the hook (see photo on page 43, "Making Fans"), chain 2, and half double crochet 1 under the same stitch you made the single crochet in. (If you want your fans really frilly, make the single crochet in the very next stitch, instead of in the 2nd from the hook.) Repeat from * for as long as you want the frill; at the end, if you need to join the edges into a round, slip stitch through the 2nd chain at the beginning (you made

Making Fans

Connecting into a Round for Circular Knitting

2 chains for height and 1 to put space between those chains and the half double crochet); or if you are making a row, end it with either a single or a half double crochet, whichever you prefer.

Knit Techniques

Knitting in the Round

Whenever you knit on a circular needle, there are 2 things to do as soon as you've cast on all your stitches:

1. Check and make sure that none of your stitches are twisted on the needle or cable. You're especially likely to twist unconsciously while knitting in the round.

2. Knit the 1st stitch of the next row with the yarn hanging from the last cast-on stitch (see photo above). This connects the stitches into a round. (It's also possible to knit *not* in the round even when knitting on a circular needle: you just skip this step.) Once this is done, you don't need to flip your work at the end of every round—and that's the whole joy of knitting in the round.

If you can't tell the beginning of your rounds from the ends (and most people can't), then you need to place a marker between the 1st and last stitches as well. I use a piece of yarn in a contrasting color (and preferably thicker than the yarn I'm knitting with—a good, healthy activity for all that leftover yarn that's just loafing about), but if you've got a marker that was manufactured just for the occasion, it's probably more convenient and certainly more considerate to put it to good use.

A lot of people I know invest in only 1 circular needle for each size (not several lengths of the same size), and you'll notice that I do all my round pieces on 32" circular needle, even when the piece is really small. How does that work, you ask? Whenever my knitting is smaller around than the cord of the needle, I just pull the cord out a little between stitches where it's connected to the right needle, so that it bunches up the stitches closer to the left needle, which makes the stitches fill up the cord. You have to adjust this every now and then as you knit, but I still think it's better than spending a small fortune on more knitting bag clutter that you can do without.

Intarsia (and Her Less Infamous Cousin, the Raised Stitch)

Likely the most feared of all knitting techniques, intarsia doesn't have to induce nightmares. Everybody's seen it, but just in case you're not familiar with the technical term, intarsia is the technique that gets purty pictures into the middle of a pattern (see photo above).

You should use it only in garments in which extra yarn won't bother you, because it makes 2 layers of yarn where you do the pattern (1 is your knitting, the 2nd is the other yarn you drag behind it until it is

Zigzag in Intarsia

used for a stitch). Summer garments are pretty much out for this technique, but winter stuff, blankets, bags, and other accessories are great candidates.

One more guideline before we get down to the knitty-gritty: use only single-color yarn (not one of the many new yarns that combine lots of colors or look tie-dyed) for intarsia, and only smooth, uniform yarn (not like Gedifra Carioca, with tails flying off it every couple of inches). It's sometimes hard for me to restrain myself in this area, but I've learned from hands-on experience that this is one law of design that you shouldn't break. You won't be pleased with the result if you do.

Intarsia is done only in stockinette stitch, and it's always done on the knit side, because if it's done on the purl side, the main color can be seen lurking behind the contrasting color in your picture. (You can do intarsia with knit stitches on the purl side, also, but they'll be indented, not raised.) Since that's about the only way you ever see it done, I'm going to give you instructions just for that. But remember that the rest of the garment can still be knit any way you want, so long as you keep the area around your intarsia in stockinette. I'm also limiting these instructions to the basic, 2-color intarsia; explaining more than that is like running a three- (or four-, or five-) ring circus.

Here we go. Have a look at the intarsia chart in your pattern. The rows you'll knit are numbered on the chart's rows; the chart's columns show the stitch number within the knitted rows. An "X" means you knit that stitch in intarsia, that is, with the yarn you're using for the picture. Pay attention to the direction you're working in as compared to that shown on the chart, lest you wind up with Rudolph in reverse.

You knit totally normally up to the point where the intarsia chart in your pattern begins. The 1st time you join new yarn for the intarsia, simply drop the yarn you were using (the main color, or **MC**), and pick up the new one (the contrasting color, or **CC**), holding it as usual. Insert the needle through the stitch you want to work the intarsia in, yarn over with the new yarn, and knit the stitch as you normally would. (That means: for a knit stitch, hold the yarn behind your work; for a purl stitch, hold it in front; see photo top right) When you switch back to **MC** yarn, drop **CC** and

Knitting with CC (as seen from wrong side)

Knitting with MC (as seen from wrong side)

Knitting with MC (as seen from right side)

pull **MC** over on top of it (see photos on page 45, "Knitting with MC [as seen from wrong side]" and "Knitting with MC [as seen from right side]"); when you need to pick up **CC** again, pull it over on top of **MC**. *Always* (always!) keep the yarn you're working with on top of the color you've dropped. If you wind up with 2 balls that look like a rat's nest and a very sloppy back to your work, it's because you didn't keep your yarns straight. If you find you're perpetually weaving a rat's nest, go buy some bobbins, or make your own out of cardboard. They'll keep you straight.

This Is Important

Each time you pick up, make sure to leave a little slack between the last stitch in **CC** and the stitch you're about to make. As you knit, the yarn will tighten up, so if you don't leave slack it's very likely that your puppies or hearts or letters or whatever will wind up puckered. How much slack to leave, you ask? At the end of every row, stretch your work a little (see page 20) and then take a look at the right side of the garment to make sure that the **CC** stitches are still the same size as the **MC** ones. You'll know right away if you pulled the yarn too tight.

A lot of up-and-coming knitters think intarsia is a little too suburban-minivan-Martha Stewart-ish. If you're one of those, the raised stitch might be more your style. Raised stitches can create a basic shape in your garment, but because they're done with the MC yarn, you don't see the whole "picture." In other

Making a Diamond in Raised Stitch

words, where intarsia can give you all the detailed shadows and hairlines and sexy curves on Elvis's face, raised stitches will just give you the King's silhouette. It's used mostly for geometric shapes, though; it's kinda' hard to see anything else. Like intarsia, raised stitches are made only on the knit side of stockinette stitch.

Because you don't have to switch yarns all the time, making raised stitches is much easier and faster than intarsia. In the middle of a knit row, you purl (see photo above); in the middle of a purl row, you knit. That's all there is to it.

To say a good word for intarsia, as I feel is my duty, it's great for expressing whatever crazy obsession you're harboring at the moment. If that obsession is

Santa Claus or reindeer or little kitty faces, so be it. But if you're obsessed with spikes and chains or Celtic symbols or the image of the Maharaji, intarsia is just as suited to that. And never underestimate the joy you could bring to your little cousin's face with a birthday sweater graced by Bambi or a couple of the Muppets—in my experience, it's well worth the effort.

These days creating your own pattern for intarsia or raised stitches is super easy. Just find an electronic file of the picture or shape you want to knit, and lay it over the rows and columns of a table in any word processing program. Number the squares for each of the stitches, print it out, and knit away.

Cables

Old but not outdated, cables can be done with endless variations, they add a lot to an otherwise boring pattern, they make winter garments even warmer by bunching the yarn together, and a lot of people think they're a blast (or at least an interesting challenge) to knit. They take a little extra equipment, a little extra counting, some extra attention, extra time, and even extra effort . . . but they're worth it all.

Cables are basically columns of stitches that get flopped around at regular intervals, which gives them a "twisted" look. Although you can snake them all over a garment, that requires a lot of planning, a lot of pieces, and a lot of sewing. (And often a lot of unraveling.) Done the simple, straight-up way, you can knit a cable only in the direction you're knitting. They're made in stockinette stitch, twisted on the knit rows, and the stitches beside them are best done in purl so that the cables stand out more. The rest of the garment, though, just as for intarsia and raised stitches, can be knit in any pattern you please.

If you're in the market for a cable, you need to decide 2 things first: (1) How many stitches wide do you want the cable to be? (Remember that each side of the cable will be only half that number.) (2) How many rows do you want between each twist? Some people think intervals that are too short make cables look stumpy, others think if you make 'em too long they look lanky. Try knitting a slim swatch with a cable in the middle, and see what you like. I'm just going to give you instructions for the basic 2-column cable. There are also braids and multiple-column cables—really hard stuff.

So, let's say you're knitting a stockinette-stitch garment that's 16 stitches wide and you want a cable in the middle that's 6 stitches wide and twisted every 6th row. If you don't have a cable needle, go get one. Then knit a few stockinette rows, and on the row where you want your cable to begin (you can just start the cable at the very bottom, if you like), purl the 1st 5 stitches, knit the next 6 to begin the cable, then purl the last 5. On the next row, knit the 1st 5 stitches, purl the next 6 for the cable, and knit the last 5. Repeat these 2 rows to create the cable in stockinette stitch until you reach the 5th row of the cable. Why the 5th? Because you have to twist the cable on a knit

Right-Twisting Cable

Step 1

Step 2

row (knit for the cables, that is, but purl for the rest of your swatch) so that it will show. After the 1st twist, you'll really twist on every 6th row.

So, on the 5th row, whip out the cable needle, purl the 1st 5 stitches, put the next 3 stitches (half the total number of stitches in the cable, since this is a 2-column cable) onto the cable needle, and *move it to the back of your work*. Holding the cable needle *behind your work* (this is super important—see step 1 above), knit the next 3 stitches that are on your left needle, then bring the cable needle back to the front of your work. (You can also place the stitches from the cable needle back on your left needle at this point, but make sure you put them back on in order, such that the last one you took off is the 1st one to go back on.

Try knitting from the cable needle first; then, the next time try putting them back on the left needle. See which method you prefer.) Knit the 3 stitches from the cable needle in order, that is, don't twist them or knit the one on the left 1st (see step 2 above). Then just purl the last 5 stitches on the row, and relax for the next 5 rows. On row 11, do it all again. And on row 17. And 23. You get the idea.

You can make the cable twist the other way by holding the cable needle *in front of your work* (see photos on page 49, "Left-Twisting Cable, Step 1" and "Left-Twisting Cable, Step 2"). If you've got 2 or more cables in a garment, it's a good idea to twist them different ways. I don't recommend twisting a single cable in opposite directions, though; it just looks

Left-Twisting Cable

Step 1

Step 2

unnatural (although some patterns do call for it). Also, when you knit the 1st set of stitches on the twist row in a cable, you'll see a big hole where you moved the last set of stitches to the cable needle. To avoid having a big strand of yarn between the 1st set and the 2nd set, knit the 1st stitch of the 2nd set very tightly against the last stitch you knitted from the 1st set, and always check that you don't have loose yarn hanging around between them.

Extended Stitches

A lot of new yarns out there are beautiful all by themselves, and manufacturers are coming up with different ones every day. You can knit these yarns without any fancy techniques or designs and they'll be some-

thing special regardless. With regular stitches, though, you generally notice the repetitive weaving of the knitting more than you do the yarn. So, when you have a yarn that can stand alone, don't cramp its style: knit it in extended stitches. Extended stitches leave a (sometimes much) longer strand of yarn in between rows, which not only means (always) less knitting for you but also lets an exceptional yarn show off its stuff.

Extended stitches also work like net by providing ventilation for summer garments—just make sure you don't use them where you wouldn't want skin to show. I use them in winter garments as well, albeit with much thicker yarns. Do keep in mind, though: if you're knitting a top, you might want to nix the

Knitting a Normal Stitch Between Yarn Overs

Unwrapping Yarn Overs

extended stitch pattern when you get to the bust, or else be prepared to wear something under it. The same goes for skirts and pants: probably best to knit the "private" section with regular stitches. If you're the last person to be described as shy, though, or if you've really got it goin' on, maybe this is the perfect stitch for you.

You can make extended stitches in just about any pattern, but knit, purl, and stockinette are best. The extended stitches will dominate the garment anyway, so it doesn't make sense to waste time getting in some complicated pattern almost no one will notice. Keep it simple, and let the extended stitches show off the yarn's natural (OK, manufactured) beauty.

There are a couple of things you should never do with extended stitches: don't start off a base row with them (base rows need to be good and sturdy), and don't put them on edges that need to be sewn together (they also need to be good and sturdy). In general, extended stitches are best on garments that don't need to be sewn, like 1-piece garments or garments knit in the round, but it is possible to sew them together, as long as you don't knit the extended stitches all the way to the edges. (Just knit the 1st and last few stitches of all the rows normally.)

To make a row of basic extended stitches, just knit 1, yarn over 1, knit another stitch, yarn over 1 more, for as far as you want those extended stitches to go. Don't skip or pass over any stitches as you yarn

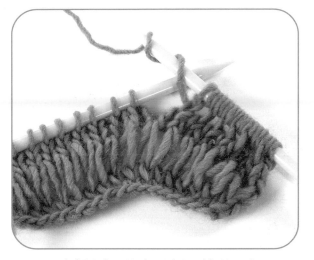

Extended Stitches Made with Double Yarn Overs

over, and don't touch the yarn overs. Leave them between the knit stitches until you get to the next row, such that you'll have a needle full of regular stitches interspersed with yarn overs (see photo on page 50, "Knitting a Normal Stitch Between Yarn Overs"). Be sure that your yarn over wraps don't accidentally jump over any of your regular stitches.

On the next row, knit 1 again, unwrap the yarned-over yarn, knit another 1, unwrap again, knit . . . you dig me. As you do this, be careful not to knit your wraps or to lose your real stitches as you unwrap (see photo on page 50, "Unwrapping Yarn Overs"). What'll you get at the end? A funky-looking row of giant Vs. The yarn you wrapped around the needle just reserved a little more space to go between rows.

After every single row you unwrap in extended stitches, you need to stretch the rows before you continue. Do it just like you do before ironing or blocking a knit (see "Blocking and All That Fun Stuff" on page 25). And don't forget to do it! Stretching is what keeps all your extended stitches nice and even in length.

You can vary the extended stitch technique a lot of ways: to make the extended stitches longer, yarn over twice in between each knitted stitch (see photo left), or even 20 times—just try it with your yarn first to make sure it'll be sturdy enough for whatever you intend to use it for.

The General Stuff

Multistranding

Knitting (or crocheting) a garment while holding several strands of yarns together makes a much sturdier piece. It also gives you an opportunity to get a few of your favorite colors into every single stitch. The texture it creates depends on the yarns you use, but whether or not the yarn reveals it, knitting with a few strands creates stitches that have a ropelike twist to them.

You can use this technique with thin yarns that you really love but that aren't warm enough for winter garments in single strands, and the multiple strands will give extra warmth. Or, you can knit holding several strands of thick yarns together for serious, off-to-Siberia warmth. Knitting with drastically different yarns held together makes for a very interesting texture and appearance (that depends on the combination, of course), and taking advantage of this fact can endow you with one of the most unusual, least duplicable wardrobes in the world.

The only thing you need to remember when knitting with several strands of yarn is that, whenever you cut the yarn, you need to knot together all the strands you held together.

Increasing and Decreasing

Count up all the ways to do these 2 basic techniques and you'll probably come out with something close to the number of sheep in Australia. In this book, however, you'll need to know only 1 way to increase in knit, 2 ways to increase in crochet, 4 ways to decrease in knit, and 2 ways to decrease in crochet. Whatever you're increasing or decreasing, the key is to do it gradually, spacing the increases or decreases evenly across the row. (Remember that, because I'll actually leave that element of design to you in one of my patterns.) This goes for both knit and crochet, both knit and purl, everything. It's just plain good design. Now, let's start with increasing, since that'll be over faster.

Increasing

I try to avoid increasing in knit entirely because it's just plain hard. It's also often easier to see increases in knit than it is to see decreases, because increasing can leave holes between stitches. That's why you'll

Increasing in Single Crochet

usually catch me casting on for the widest part of just about anything and then decreasing my way down. Still, sometimes you can't get around it.

The only time you'll ever increase in knit in this book is by casting on for buttonholes, so when you get that far, turn to the buttonholes section of this chapter (page 55) to figure out how to do it.

Increasing in crochet happens almost automatically. You'll do it in practically every crochet pattern in this book, and if I didn't tell you what you were doing, you wouldn't even notice it. All you have to do is crochet more than 1 stitch in the stitch you're crocheting through on the previous row (see photo above). If you're making a pattern (like shells, fans, or net), you just put more chain stitches between each end point (the sides of the shell or fan, or the columns that form the sides of a rectangle in net).

Decreasing Along Edge in Knit

Decreasing Along Edge in Purl

Decreasing

Decreasing in knit provides a lot of opportunities for attractive shaping. You've probably noticed that already while you decreased for necklines. Here's what you need to know to get the most attractive decreases for my patterns:

On edges (such as around armholes or necklines), I almost always decrease by simply binding off the 1st or last stitch(es) on the row. You can do this in knit or purl (see photos above), and it's fast and easy, so I think it's the best way. This is the decrease you'll use to make all buttonholes as well. It's really easy.

In the middle of a garment, I decrease by knitting 2 stitches together, which is exactly what you do when you bind off (only on a smaller scale). You can do this in knit or purl as well, but do it only with yarn that doesn't betray the decrease (or only when you

don't care if people see it). I use a lot of puffy, wacky yarns, so this is a good one for me. It's not so great for clean, slim, 100% cotton yarns that knit up tight and straight, because they show everything.

The next 2 methods can be used for any yarn, and they can be done in both knit and purl. They're a bit trickier than the others, though, so you'll do them only in knit, which is the easier way. Why are they harder? As you decrease, you have to simultaneously make your decrease slant left or right. This can make really nice slashlike stitches that add to the design of a garment, provided you slant them the right way every time.

To make a left-slanting decrease, just pass the stitch you want to decrease onto the right needle without knitting it. Knit the next stitch that's on the left needle as usual (see photo on page 54, "Making a Left-Slanting Decrease, Step 1"). Once you've got that

Step 1

Making a Left-Slanting Decrease

Step 2

Making a Left-Slanting Decrease

Making a Right-Slanting Decrease

stitch on the right needle, insert the left needle into the front of the slipped stitch, and hop it over the knitted stitch (see step 2 left) and off the needle. This is abbreviated skp (slip knit pass), but we'll use it only a couple of times in the book.

To make a right-slanting decrease, insert the needle from behind through both the 1st and 2nd stitches on the end of the needle (see photo bottom left), yarn over, pull the yarn through both stitches, and slide them off the left needle, leaving the single new stitch on the right needle.

Decreasing in crochet is as easy as increasing. In fact, it really is just increasing backwards: just skip over stitches on the previous row (see photo below) or, if you're crocheting a pattern (shells, fans, net, or the like), make fewer chains between the 2 end points of the pattern (the sides of shells or fans, the 2 columns that form the sides of a rectangle in net). I recommend that you skip over only 1 stitch at a time,

Decreasing in Single Crochet

Making a Buttonhole

1st row

2nd row

though, otherwise you're too likely to stretch the yarn, which will bunch up your crocheting.

And once more (say it with me, kids), the Golden Rule of all increasing and decreasing is: do it gra-du-al-ly!

Buttonholes

All the buttonholes in this book are made by a 2-step process: on the 1st row of the buttonhole, you make a left-slanting decrease (which binds off a stitch, as in the photo above), and on the 2nd row you cast that stitch back on.

You already know how to make a left-slanting decrease (if you skipped it, see the preceding section), but casting on a stitch in the middle of a row is

admittedly a bit of a challenge, so look closely at the photo above. It really is exactly like casting on at the very beginning of a piece (see page 9), except that you have only 1 strand of yarn instead of 2. Otherwise all the fingerwork is the same.

Picking Up Stitches and Building On

Despite all the praise I showered upon crochet for its ability to create crazy shapes, sometimes it's easiest to just knit a piece as a rectangle and then build onto it any "peripherals" necessary to fit your body. (This is not sewing 2 already-knit pieces together. I'm talking about building a new piece up directly from a piece you've already knit.) Building onto a piece is the best way to go about connecting 2 pieces that are different

Building On with Slip Stitches

Building On with Single Crochet Stitches

sizes (like a smaller waist on a much wider skirt), and we'll use it constantly.

You can use this technique as well to build knitting or crocheting onto different materials. Any material that you can punch holes in without destroying (or that already has sturdy holes) you can attach knitting and crocheting to. For instance, I build up a lot from leather, you'll build up from rubber clogs in this book, and you can do it on other stuff, as well, like hemp, soft wicker (the kind some bags are made of), or woven materials. Cotton cloth or anything delicate will just fall apart. (Cheesecloth, for instance, has holes, but they won't hold your knitting.)

To build on from another knit piece, you bind off your work as usual, then go back to pick up the stitches you want to build from (not necessarily the

bound-off edge), and begin working in a new direction. Once you have all the stitches you want to build from on your needle or hook, just start stitching as usual. This is really easy, as long as you know the back of a stitch from the front. Study the pictures about picking up long and hard, if need be.

There are a few ways to build on, depending upon what you're building from and whether you're doing it in knit or crochet. When you crochet a special row just to build from (you'll do that often), use slip stitches (see photo above left) if you're doing it from within a base material (like the center of a leather belt or around the middle of a wicker basket), because slip stitches are very inflexible, so they'll hold your knitting tightly onto the material. If you're building up from an edge, however, (whether it's knitting, crocheting, or even the edge of a different material), use single crochet stitches, which are more flexible than slip stitches (see photo on page 56, "Building On with Single Crochet Stitches").

If your foundation stitches are slip stitches, you want to pick them up in crochet by building the next row from under the entire slip stitch. That means you'll insert your hook under the stitch, not through it, and stitch from there (see photo top right). To pick up from slip stitches in knit, though, insert the needle through either the front or the back of the slip stitch, but not both (see photo center right). Inserting through the front makes the foundation slip stitches invisible; inserting through the back leaves the front part of the foundation visible.

If you've got a foundation of single crochets, pick up for crochet by inserting the hook in the single crochet stitch itself. To pick up for knit, insert through the front or back only (see photo bottom right). (The same front-back visibility rule applies here as for building from slip stitches.)

No matter how you're picking up or from what foundation, pay attention and be extra careful that the stitches don't twist as you slide them onto the needle or hook. This is especially likely to occur when you're picking up stitches.

You'll use this technique a lot in this book. Eventually you won't need to look up which way to do what anymore. Most people catch on to the hows and whys of this really fast.

Picking Up Slip Stitches for Crochet

Picking Up Slip Stitches for Knit

Picking Up Single Crochet Stitches (through back leg) for Knit

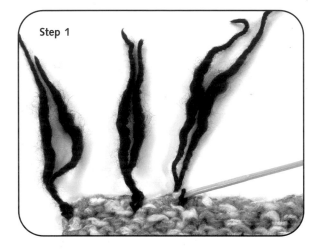

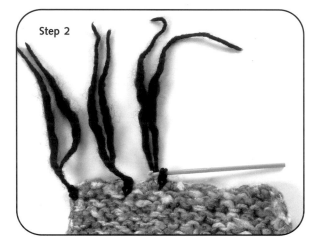

Attaching Fringes

Fringes are probably the most common addition to any knitted garment. There are a lot of ways to put fringes on, and they're all easy. Here's my favorite: Attach them with your garment right side up and right side out; otherwise they seem to bulge off the edge. It's also a really good idea to figure out exactly where you want to attach them (maybe even safety-pin the spot) before you start putting the fringes on — unevenly spaced fringes are a bit of an eyesore. If you're putting them along a straight edge, fold the edge in half and mark the center, then the corners, then space the rest evenly between.

Prepare your fringes by cutting however many pieces of yarn you need, making sure that they're twice as long as the fringes you want. (You can, of course, fold your fringes so that 1 side of each will hang shorter than the other when attached to the garment. In that case, measure your yarn however you need to before you cut it.) Fold a piece of yarn to make 2 strands that hang down together. Insert a crochet hook (whatever size fits through your knitting or crochet) from above through a stitch or hole on the edge of the garment, hook the fringe through its fold, and pull the fold up through the hole to the right side of the garment (see step 1 above). Hook around both strands hanging beyond the edge, and make a slip stitch to fasten the fringe to the garment (see step 2 above), then chain 1 to make a knot on the edge. Tighten the knot to make sure the fringe won't fall off.

Weaving in Straps and Ties

As far as this book is concerned, you'll weave straps and ties into only a crocheted edging. Weaving in straps (such as a neck strap on a bikini, or shoulder straps on a tank top) and ties (such as in the waist of a skirt or pants, or around the top of a bag) can give a garment or accessory more of a down-to-earth, homemade look, and can add interesting texture you can't get out of yarn no matter how you knit it. (It can also save you a hell of a lot of knitting. But that's just a side benefit.) I'm a big bovine buff, so I use thin strips of leather, but you can use any type of rope or fabric or lace or thick, sturdy string—even twine, if you can bear the itching.

You can technically weave stuff through knitting, but I don't recommend it. Weaving through knit stitches is likely to destroy the yarn. It's easier to weave through crocheting anyway (especially on edges), because crocheting leaves clear holes between stitches. In fact, in most of my patterns, I add on a special element I call "windows" (see more at the beginning of this chapter), which places plenty of space between stitches I intend to weave through (see photo above). It's a little extra work, but it's the best way to protect your multi-material knit from itself.

Whatever it is you're using, weave it in using a crochet hook (whichever size will fit through your edge stitches). If it's a tie that you're going to be opening and closing a lot, make sure to insert it at the point where you'll want to tie it: like on the outside of

Weaving In through Windows

a foothole, or on the front of the waist. (If it's something that you'll just tie once and never undo, like a neck or shoulder strap, don't worry about it.) If you're weaving it in along a straight edge (the waist, the foot hole, the top of a bag), make sure to fold the edge in half to find the exact center or side between front and back. If it's not a straight edge (an arm opening in a tank top, for instance), just make sure you start in the very top corner stitch, otherwise that stitch will just hang there limp underneath your strap.

Continue weaving by using the crochet hook to pull the material back and forth through the holes along the edge. You can skip a few "windows" (holes, stitches, whatever) between weave-ins if you don't want the edge to bunch up too much when you tie it. Remember this if you ever knit for a "manly man": if you don't skip stitches, as soon as he ties that thing closed he's going to feel like a frilly sissy.

Remember what I said at the beginning of this chapter about "every other design you'll ever see" being "at your creative mercy"? Let me qualify that just a bit: When I go to the yarn store, I still occasionally see some old lady's hands flying in directions I never imagined. But whenever I ask myself, "How the hell did she do *that?*" I always make sure to ask her, too. And always, after a little chat, a few cookies, a few times of saying "Wait, do that again," it suddenly seems like common sense.

So, even if you learn these elements inside out and backwards, you'll still run across things now and then that totally blow your mind. Ask. Knitting has been a social activity since the first sock was stitched thousands of years ago, and some of the coolest, most unbelievable stuff has been passed down from old Hungarian or Venezuelan or Mandarin grandmas for generations without ever finding their way into a book. Even if you're like me and prefer to knit in solitude, be sure to keep an eye out for what your fellow knitters are doing, and kick-start the small talk if it's something you don't recognize. This book should give you the foundation to understand it, and it could wind up making the most awesome socks in your drawer.

CHAPTER FOUR

Designs from Head to Toe

As you'll notice, the designs in this book are pretty unconventional. It was primarily city life and fashion that gave birth to my love of wacky yarns and crazy urban styles, but my childhood memories (and childish adult obsessions) are usually the source of my ideas. Now that I live in the city and have learned to indulge my "inner child," I find myself perpetually inspired, by clothes in shop windows (or on people's bodies), by characters in fairy tales, movies, and cartoons—even by shapes I see on buildings or around the house. If you see the beauty in everything around you, too, you'll never want for knitting and crocheting ideas. Have a look at the designs that follow and you'll see how it works.

Beach Bandana

Back when I was trying a knit version of everything in sight, a day at the beach challenged me to create this design. It's more delicate than bandanas made of fabric, so it looks cool wrapped around your waist as well.

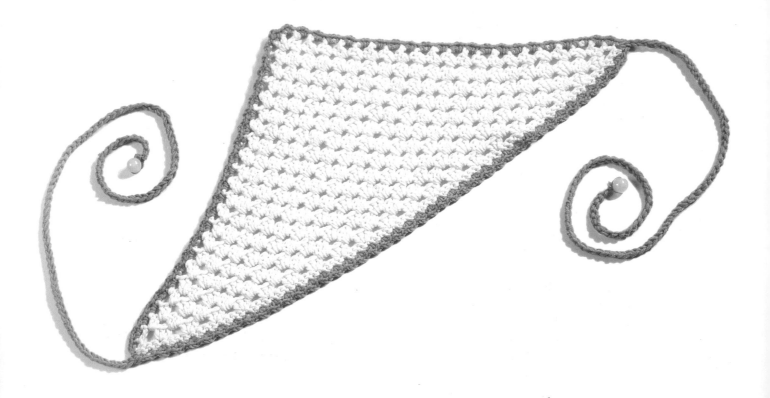

Overview

The bandana is crocheted entirely in a shell pattern, from the wide base of the triangle. On each row, you decrease $1/2$ shell on each end until you taper to the triangle's point. Once that's done, you add a border, stitch up the ties, and tie them. Remember to flip your garment after each row!

Directions

Base Row With **A**, ch 84.

Row 1 Ch 1 to move up from base of triangle (that is, to build height of row), then sc 84 to end.

Row 2

1. Ch 2 for height, then dc 1 in 1st st of prev row (ignoring the 2 ch you just made).

2. *Ch 1, then dc 3, all in 4th st from hook (4th st from your previous dc); rep from * 19x—20 shells (sets of dc 3) total.

3. Ch 1 and dc 2 in last st of prev row. Turn your work.

Row 3

1. Ch 3—2 for height, 1 for width.

2. Dc 2 around—not through—the ch betw the 1st and 2nd shells (the ch above the hole).

3. *Ch 1 and dc 3 around—not through— ch above next hole betw shells; rep from * 18x—19 shells total.

4. Ch 1 and dc 2 in the last hole; then ch 1 and dc 1 through the last st on prev row.

Rows 4–21 For these 18 rows, repeat row 3, but make 1 fewer shell in step 3 each row. In other words, for row 4, repeat the pattern to make 18 shells total. By the time you reach row 21, you'll make only 1 complete and 2 half-shells.

Row 22 Ch 3—2 for height, 1 for width, then dc 2 through hole betw shells, ch 1, dc 2 through hole betw shells, ch 1, and dc 1 through the last st. (You should have only 2 half shells.)

Row 23 Ch 3, dc 2 through hole, ch 1, and dc 1 through the last st. (Just 1 half shell.)

FO

Crochet Border: Fans

The 2 sides of the bandana are exactly the same, but choose one now to be the "right" side for the rest of the crocheting. Lay the bandana with the right side facing up.

1. Fold over end of **B**, and hold it below right corner of triangle's base. Insert your hook from above through 1st ch you made, pull yarn through the st, and ch 3; then hdc 1 through same 1st st in the corner.

Crocheting the Border

2. *Sc 1 through 2nd st from hook, ch 2, hdc 1 in same st; rep from * every 2nd st to end of triangle's base—42x total.

Unlike the base, the sides of your triangle are made up both of ch sts and dc sts. Not a problem. Just repeat step 2 all around the bandana's edge, crocheting in the holes below chains where you've got them, and in the holes below double crochets where you've got those instead (see photo, "Crocheting the border").

3. Cont to rep step 2 along next side of triangle. *Don't crochet through sts themselves!* At top of bandana, where you have only 1 ch betw 2 dc, make your sts in hole betw dc (around ch).

4. When you reach bottom right corner of triangle again, pull your yarn through 2nd ch you made at beg of border, FO, and hide tail in border.

Crochet Ties

If you find it too difficult to chain 2 strands together with such a small hook, use a 3 or 4 mm hook instead. To prepare the ties, cut two 20-foot pieces of **B** and fold each in half (you'll work as if holding 2 strands of yarn together, only they're connected here).

1. Lay your bandana RS up in front of you, and place 1 piece of folded yarn with fold under 1 corner of base. Insert your hook from above betw white and orange yarns at corner, hook the fold in the yarn, and pull a loop through.

2. Insert hook through corner st (in orange border) and sl st 1. This fastens yarn into place.

3. Holding both strands of folded-over yarn tog, ch 80–90 (depending upon how long you want your ties to be, which depends largely on the size of your noggin).

4. Pull yarn through, knot it, thread 1 of your beads onto yarn (using a sewing needle or threader will make this easier), and knot yarn several times more to fasten it tight. FO.

Rep for other tie.

The simple crocheted triangle is also good for making shawls. For a shawl, though, you'll want to use thicker yarns (and hence a bigger hook) to make it warm for the winter. Otherwise, you can follow this pattern exactly—just as long as you can do the math. I'll help you this time, so you can wing it next winter.

The width of each shell is 3 double crochets plus 1 chain, which means that it takes up the width of 4 chains of the base row. (All stitches crocheted with the same yarn and hook have the same width, remember?) You need an even number of shells on the 1st row in order to keep the angles of the triangle the same. An even number of 4-stitch-wide shells means the number of chains you make has to be divisible by 8 (every 2 whole shells on the 1st row take 8 stitches), and then you have to add the 2 half shells that will decrease the edges, too, so you add 4 more chains.

How do you know how wide you want the shawl to be? The easiest way to find out is simply to make a bunch of chain stitches for the base row. When you've got it pretty long, continue until the number is divisible by 8, and then add another 4 chain stitches. Now try wrapping it around your shoulders. If it's wide enough for you, start crocheting the pattern, decreasing by 1 repetition on each row, just as you did for the bandana. If it's not wide enough, continue the chains to the next number divisible by 8, add 4, and try again.

1920s Cloche Hat

The "flapper hat," as it's often called, is actually a cloche hat. It works best with short, cropped hair, which was the style in the 1920s. The same goes for this hat. If you're a flapper kind of girl, make this and the Charleston Tank Top in matching colors.

Overview

The hat is crocheted in rounds, each one connected at the end with a slip stitch. In case I ever forget to tell you: on a single crochet row, slip stitch 1 through the chain at the beginning; on a double crochet row, slip stitch 1 through the 2nd chain at the beginning. You'll crochet from the top down, increasing width as you build length.

Directions

Base Rnd With A, ch 5, then sl st 1 through 1st ch to close row into a ring.

Rnd 1 Sc 8 through ring (not ch sts themselves), then sl st 1 under 1st sc on the rnd.

Rnds 2–3: Making the Top Knob Ch 1, then sc 1 through each sc (the sts themselves) on rnd 1—7 sc total + 1 ch; sl st 1 under ch at beg of rnd.

Rnd 4

1. Ch 2 for height, and dc 1 in same st on prev rnd.

2. Dc 2 in each foll sc—15 dc total + 2 ch; sl st 1 through 2nd ch at beg of rnd. You just inc 8 sts.

Rnd 5

1. Drop A and join B, ch 1, sc 2 in next st (the 1st dc of rnd 4).

2. *Sc 1 in next st, sc 2 in next st; rep from * to end—23 sc total + 1 ch; sl st 1 through ch at beg of rnd. You inc 8 more sts.

Rnd 6: Fans

1. Drop B and pick up A, ch 2, dc 1 in next st, dc 2 in foll st.

2. *Dc 1 in next 2 sts, dc 2 in 3rd st; rep from * (sets of 3) to end—31 dc total + 2 ch; sl st 1 in 2nd ch at beg of rnd. You inc 8 sts.

Rnd 7

1. Drop **A** and pick up **B**, ch 1, sc 1 in next 2 sts, sc 2 in 3rd st.

2. Work in sets of 4: *sc 1 in next 3 sts, then sc 2 in 4th st; rep from * to end—39 sc total + 1 ch; sl st 1 in ch at beg of rnd. You inc 8 sts.

Rnd 8

1. Drop **B** and pick up **A**, ch 2, dc 1 in each of next 3 sts, and dc 2 in foll st.

2. Work in sets of 5: *dc 1 in 1st 4 sts, then dc 2 in 5th st; rep from * to end—47 dc total + 2 ch; sl st 1 in 2nd ch at beg of rnd. You inc 8 sts.

Rnd 9 Drop **A** and pick up **B**, ch 1, sc 1 in each st to end—47 sc total + 1 ch; sl st 1 in ch at beg of rnd.

Rnd 10

1. With **B**, ch 2, dc 1 in each of next 5 sts, and dc 2 in foll st.

2. Cont working in sets of 6: *dc 1 in 1st 5 sts, then dc 2 in 6th; rep from * to end—55 dc total + 2 ch; sl st 1 in 2nd ch at beg of rnd. You inc 8 sts.

Rnd 11 Drop **B** and pick up **A**, ch 1, sc 1 in each st to end—55 sc total + 1 ch; sl st 1 in ch at beg of rnd, and cut **A**.

Rnd 12: Windows

1. With **B**, ch 4—2 for height and 2 for length.

2. *Hdc 1 in 2nd st from hook, ch 2; rep from * to end—27x total; sl st 1 in 2nd ch at beg of rnd.

Rnd 13 With **B**, ch 1, then sc 2 through each hole (under the 2 ch sts that connect the windows, not through the sts themselves) on the prev rnd, and sc 1 in each hdc—83 sc total + 1 ch; sl st 1 in ch at beg of rnd.

Rnd 14 Drop **B** and join **C**, ch 1, sc 1 in each sc on prev rnd—83 sc total + 1 ch; sl st 1 in ch at beg of rnd.

Rnd 15: Windows You crochet this round just like round 12, but you make 1 ch fewer each time. (It just makes the space between your holes smaller.) So:

1. With **C**, ch 3—2 for height and 1 for length.

2. *Hdc 1 in 2nd st from hook, ch 1; rep from * to end—41x total; sl st 1 in 2nd ch at beg of rnd.

Rnd 16: Fans Drop **C** and pick up **B**. Rep foll patt in each hole (under the ch that connects the windows, not through the ch itself) on rnd 15: sc 1 through hole, ch 2, hdc 1 in same hole—41x total; sl st 1 in 1st sc at beg of rnd.

Rnd 17: Windows

1. Drop **B** and pick up **C**, sl st 1 in hole betw 1st sc and hdc of rnd 16 (center of 1st fan), and ch 4—2 for height and 2 for width.

2. *Hdc 1 through center of next fan, ch 2; rep from * to end—41x total; sl st 1 in 2nd ch at beg of rnd; cut **C**.

Rnd 18: Shells With **B**, sl st 1 through 1st hole (under the 2 ch sts, not through the sts themselves), ch 2, dc 1 in same hole; then dc 2 in each foll hole to end—83 dc total + 2 ch; sl st 1 in 2nd ch at beg of rnd.

Rnd 19

1. Drop **B** and join **A**, then ch 1, sc 1 in each of next 5 sts, and sc 2 in 6th.

2. Work in sets of 7: *sc 1 in each of 1st 6 sts, then sc 2 in 7th; rep from * to end—11x total, 95 sc total + 1 ch; sl st 1 in ch at beg of rnd. You inc 12 sts.

Rnd 20 Drop **A** and pick up **B**, then ch 2 and dc 1 in each st to end—95 dc total + 2 ch; sl st 1 in 2nd ch at beg of rnd.

Rnd 21

S: Rep rnd 20.

M (L):

1. With **B**, ch 2, dc 1 in each of next 14 (6) sts, and dc 2 in 15th (7th) st.

2. Now work in sets of 16 (8): *dc 1 in each of 1st 15 (7) sts, then dc 2 in 16th (8th); rep from * to end— 5x (11x) total, 101 (107) dc total; sl st 1 in 2nd ch at beg of rnd. You inc 6 (12) sts.

Rnd 22 With **B**, ch 2 and dc 1 in each st to end—95 (101, 107) dc total + 2 ch; sl st 1 in 2nd ch at beg of rnd.

Rnd 23 Drop **B** and pick up **A**; then ch 1 and sc 1 in each st to end—95 (101, 107) sc total + 1 ch; sl st 1 in ch at beg of rnd.

Rnds 24–26 Drop **A** and pick up **B**; then ch 2 and dc 1 in each st to end—95 (101, 107) dc total + 2 ch; sl st 1 in 2nd ch at beg of rnd.

Rnd 27 Rep rnd 23.

Rnds 28–29 Rep rnd 24, then cut **B**.

Rnd 30: Sneaky Peeking Rnd Pick up **A** and ch 2, *yo, insert your hook from below the hat into the hole betw the 2 ch sts and the 1st dc column on prev rnd, then insert hook in next hole so that 1st dc column is now behind hook (see photo on page 70, "Sneaky Peeking Round, Step 1"), yo again, pull yarn through both holes (see photo on page 70, "Sneaky Peeking

Sneaky Peeking Round

Step 1

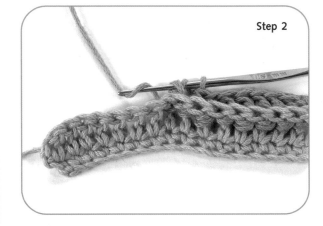

Step 2

Round, Step 2"), and dc 1. Rep from * to end of rnd—95 (101, 107) dc total + 2 ch; sl st 1 in 2nd ch at beg of rnd.

What you just did was basically a *purl* double crochet. It places the stitches behind a row, so that the row is forced forward. It creates the appearance that something is sneaking around behind the row—in this case, the something is peeking out from underneath the hat. You can use this technique the other way around as well (just insert the hook from above the garment and then up into the next hole/stitch so that the column is in front of the hook); or you can alternate "purl" and "knit" for a "ribbed" look in crochet. You can't purl or knit on single crochets, though, because you need columns—only double crochets or more.

Rnd 31: Fans

1. Drop **A** and join **C**; ch 3, and hdc 1 in same st on prev rnd.

2. *Sc 1 in 2nd st from hook, ch 2, hdc 1 in same st as sc; rep from * to end—47x (50x, 53x) total; sl st 1 in 2nd ch at beg of rnd and cut **C**.

Rnd 32: Fans

1. Pick up **A** and sl st 1 in hole betw 1st sc and hdc of rnd 31 (center of 1st fan), ch 3, and hdc 1 in same hole.

2. *Sc 1 in center of next fan, ch 2, hdc 1 in same hole as sc; rep from * to end—47x (50x, 53x) total; sl st 1 in 2nd ch at beg of rnd.

FO… and exhale.

Kremlin Beret

What most people think are the onion domes of the Kremlin are actually the domes of St. Basil's Basilica on Red Square. But the Kremlin is better known (by name, at least), and it does have similar domes, so this beret gets its shape and its name from that edifice.

Overview

You crochet the beret from the top down, increasing as you go. Decreasing for sizes is done only in the band around the bottom. You'll make a few rows of shells in the middle, but otherwise there's nothing to it.

Directions

Base Rnd With **B**, ch 6 and sl st 1 through 1st ch to connect sts into a ring.

Rnd 1 Sc 8 through hole in ring (not through the ch sts themselves), and sl st 1 through 1st st to connect the sts into a rnd.

From now on, I'll ask you to count your double crochets at the end of each round. The 1st 3 chains at the beginning of each round substitute for a double crochet (which you need to build height for the row) so be sure to count those chains as 1 of your double crochets.

Rnd 2

1. Join **A** and ch 4, then dc 1 through 1st sc of prev rnd and ch 1.

2. *Dc 1 through next sc on prev rnd and ch 1; rep from * to end of rnd—7x total.

3. Sl st 1 through 3rd ch on this row to connect the sts into a rnd. Count to make sure you have 8 dc on this rnd. (Remember to include the 3 ch that substitute for a dc at beg of rnd.)

Rnd 3 Now you begin to inc width by making 2 dcs in each dc on prev rnd.

1. Ch 4, dc 1 through same st, and ch 1.

2. *Insert hook in next dc, and dc 1, ch 1, dc 1, ch 1—all through same dc on prev row. Rep from * to end of rnd—7x total.

3. Sl st 1 in 3rd ch at beg of this row to connect the sts into a rnd. Count to make sure you have 16 dc (including 1st 3 ch) on this rnd.

Rnd 4

1. Ch 4, then dc 1 and ch 1 through each dc on prev rnd—15x total.

2. Sl st 1 in 3rd ch at beg of this row to make a rnd. You should have 16 dc (including 1st 3 ch) on this rnd. (Obviously you didn't inc on this rnd.)

Rnd 5 Rep rnd 3 (to inc width again) but 15x total. You should have 32 dc on this rnd.

Rnds 6–7 Rep rnd 4 (to maintain current width) but 31x total. You should have 32 dc.

Rnd 8 Until now, you've increased the width of the hat by increasing in every double crochet on the previous round. On this round, however, you're going to increase only in every 4th double crochet. I'll write it out just so you're clear.

1. Ch 4, dc 1 in 1st dc of prev rnd, ch 1, dc 1 in next dc, ch 1; in next dc of prev rnd, dc 1, ch 1, dc 1, ch 1—all through the same st.

2. *Dc 1 and ch 1 in each of next 3 dc of prev rnd; in 4th dc of prev rnd, dc 1, ch 1, dc 1, ch 1; rep from * to end of rnd.

3. Sl st 1 through 3rd ch at beg of rnd. You created 8 inc. Count to make sure you have 40 dc on this rnd.

Rnds 9–10 Rep rnd 4 but 39x total. You should have 40 dc on these rnds.

Rnd 11: Shells

1. Ch 3, dc 1 in same st, ch 2, dc 2, ch 1—all through the same st.

2. *Skip 1 dc in prev rnd, then dc 2, ch 2, dc 2, ch 1—all through the same dc in prev rnd; rep from * to end of row—19x total.

3. Sl st 1 through 3rd ch at beg of this rnd. You should have 20 shells.

Rnds 12–16: Shells

1. Sl st 2 to climb up to center of 1st shell, then sl st 1 under (not through) the 2 ch sts in center of that shell.

2. Ch 3, dc 1, ch 2, dc 2—all under (not through) the 2 ch sts that join the 2 dc sides of 1st shell; ch 1 more.

3. *Dc 2, ch 2, dc 2—all under the 2 ch that join sides of next shell; ch 1 more; rep from * to end of rnd—19x total.

4. Sl st 1 in 3rd ch at beg of this rnd. You should have 20 shells on each of these rnds.

Rnd 17: Shells

1. Sl st 2 to climb up to center of 1st shell, then sl st 1 under the 2 ch sts in center of shell.

2. Ch 3, dc 1, ch 2, dc 2—all under the 2 ch that join the sides of 1st shell.

You won't make a chain between the shells here and those in step 3. That makes this row decrease just a bit.

3. *Dc 2, ch 2, dc 2—all under the 2 ch that join the sides of next shell; rep from * to end of rnd—19x total.

4. Sl st 1 in 3rd ch at beg of this rnd. You should have 20 shells on this rnd.

Rnd 18

1. Join **B** and ch 1, then sc 1 in each dc on prev rnd. Just skip over the 2 ch that connect the sides of shells.

2. Sl st 1 in 1st ch on this rnd. Count to make sure you have 80 sc on this rnd.

Rnd 19

Now here's where size matters:

S: Ch 1, *sc 1 through next 9 sc on prev rnd, skip 10th st on prev rnd; rep from * to end of rnd—72 sc total; sl st 1 in 1st ch of rnd.

M: Work same as for S, but skip each 20th st—76 sc total.

L: Work same as for S, too, but don't skip any—80 sc total.

Rnds 20–24 Ch 1, then sc 1 through each sc on prev rnd—71 (75, 79) sc + 1 ch; sl st 1 in 1st ch of rnd.

FO You're all done, comrade.

Fargo-with-a-Kiss Hat

I really dug those flappy winter hats in the movie *Fargo*, but the way they fit around the top of the head was too unimaginative. I kept an eye out for interesting shapes for a few days and eventually hit upon the Hershey's Kiss. (That'd look good on your head, right?) This hybrid design is sturdy enough for even a Minnesota winter and much easier on the hips than Hershey's.

Overview

You knit the hat in stockinette stitch from the bottom up, so you'll be decreasing (instead of increasing, as you usually do for a hat). The decreases make 4 lines around the hat that look something like seams, but I call them "Christmas trees," because each one is a vertical braid with "needles" (like the needles of a fir tree) descending from it on either side. The "needles" are the decreases, 2 different kinds, so that both are descending; indeed, 1 decrease has to slant left, and the other has to slant right. (If you don't know how to control the direction of your decreases, see page 52.) You'll decrease 8 stitches on each knit (odd) row beginning at row 7. Then you'll stitch the hat up and add the crochet bottom and flaps, the crochet edging around the flaps, and the chin ties. Just in case you want to stitch up the hole at the top of the hat, I'll tell you a few ways to do that when you're all done.

Directions

Base Row With knitting needles and **A**, CO 64 sts.

Rows 1–6 Knit St st, beg with a k row.

Row 7 As you K across, dec by knitting these sts tog, slanting in direction indicated in parentheses:

2 and 3 (right)	16 and 17 (left)
19 and 20 (right)	30 and 31 (left)
33 and 34 (right)	48 and 49 (left)

51 and 52 (right)   62 and 63 (left)
You dec 8 sts, so you should have 56 rem. (Count!)

Row 8 P to end to cont in St st.

Row 9 As you k across, dec by knitting these sts tog, slanted as indicated:

2 and 3 (right)	14 and 15 (left)
17 and 18 (right)	26 and 27 (left)
29 and 30 (right)	42 and 43 (left)
45 and 46 (right)	54 and 55 (left)

You dec 8 sts, so you should have 48 sts at the end.

Row 10 P to end to cont in St st.

Row 11 As you k across, dec by knitting these sts tog:

2 and 3 (right)	12 and 13 (left)
15 and 16 (right)	22 and 23 (left)
25 and 26 (right)	36 and 37 (left)
39 and 40 (right)	46 and 47 (left)

You should have 40 sts rem.

Row 12 P to end.

Row 13 As you k across, dec these sts:

2 and 3 (right)	10 and 11 (left)
13 and 14 (right)	18 and 19 (left)
21 and 22 (right)	30 and 31 (left)
33 and 34 (right)	38 and 39 (left)

You should have 32 sts rem.

Row 14 P to end.

Row 15 As you k, dec these sts:

2 and 3 (right)	8 and 9 (left)
11 and 12 (right)	14 and 15 (left)
17 and 18 (right)	24 and 25 (left)
27 and 28 (right)	30 and 31 (left)

You should have 24 sts rem.

Row 16 P to end.

Row 17 As you k, dec these sts:

2 and 3 (right)	6 and 7 (left)
13 and 14 (right)	18 and 19 (left)

You should have 20 sts rem. (I didn't forget anything; you're decreasing from only 2 sides instead of 4 now, because you don't have a whole lot of stitches left.)

Row 18 P to end.

Row 19 As you k, dec these sts:

2 and 3 (right)	4 and 5 (left)
11 and 12 (right)	14 and 15 (left)

You have 16 sts rem.

Row 20 P to end.

Row 21 As you k, dec these sts:

2 and 3 (right)	6 and 7 (left)
10 and 11 (right)	14 and 15 (left)

You have 12 sts rem.

BO in p.

Stitch Up

To stitch the 2 sides of the hat together, use the **A** yarn and the larger crochet hook. Here's a tip: pull a few of the fibers out of the stitching-up yarn before you start sewing, because you don't want the seam to bulge too much against your head. (Make sure the sewing yarn stays strong, though.)

1. Turn hat WS out (purl side out), and pull outside ends of hat together, so that last sts along each edge line up. Pull stitching-up yarn through 1st and last CO sts, and sl st 1.

2. Sl st edges tog, inserting hook betw 1st and 2nd sts of each row, to the top. Make sure your hook goes through both edges of hat or you're not really stitching them together.

If you turn the hat right side out and can't see the Christmas tree decreases, you stitched it up too far into the rows. Undo it, look closely, and try to insert your hook between the 1st and 2nd stitches of each row.

Crochet Bottom

Turn the hat right side out, and whip out the **B** yarn. This will be a breeze.

1. Insert your larger hook betw 1st and last CO sts (where you stitched them tog), and pull yarn through.

2. Ch 1, then sc 1 in each foll st—64 sc + 1 ch; sl st 1 under ch at beg of rnd.

3. Rep step 2 to make 7 rows total. Before you complete these rows, try the hat on, and adjust last rows to fit hat better, if necessary: To make hat a little smaller, do fewer than 64 scs (skip a st at even intervals). To make it bigger, do more than 1 sc in a few holes evenly spaced around bot edge of hat. When it fits just right, FO.

Crochet Flaps

Keep the hat right side out from now on, and watch where your seam falls: at the end of all this, it should run right smack down the center of your noggin. Pay attention to that when you count stitches in order to space the flaps evenly around. Also, all your flaps will be attached to the 6th (that's the next-to-last) row of the crocheted bottom (see photo on page 79, "Flaps"). You'll need **C** and the larger hook for all three flaps.

Front Flap

On either side of the front of the hat, you have a Christmas tree. Counting from just inside the braids, there are 17 stitches across the front. The flap is 13, so you need to leave 2 stitches on either side of it (check the picture again if you need to). Find the stitch in the crochet bottom that you're going to insert the hook into, mark it if you need to; then place the hat with the top point facing you so that you can work comfortably along the base.

1. Insert hook in sc on 6th row of crocheted bottom, yo, pull yarn through to top, then sl st 1 through each of foll 13 sc; FO.

2. Join **C** again, and insert your hook under 1st sl st of prev row, ch 1, then sc 1 under each foll sl st to end—12 sc + 1 ch.

3. *On next row, ch 1 and sc to end; rep from * 4x to make a total of 5 rows.

In the next 2 rows you'll decrease by simply skipping the 2nd and next-to-last stitches of the row:

4. *Ch 1, sc 1 in 2nd st from hook, sc 10, skip next st, and sc 1 in last st; rep from * , but sc 8 in middle, to make a total of 2 dec rows.

5. Sl st 1 somewhere along edge (don't force yarn to go where it doesn't want to) to fasten down yarn, then FO.

Side Flaps

Now you'll do more or less the same thing along the sides. Between the Christmas trees on the sides, you have 13 stitches, and the side flaps will be 11, hence 1 stitch in from either side (you can also see this in the photo, "Flaps").

1. Join **C**. On 6th row of crocheted bottom, make row of sl st. FO—just as you did for front flap.

2. Join yarn again, and sc 15 rows, then dec, skipping 2nd and next-to-last sts) on rows 16–18.

Flaps

Since each side flap is only 11 sts (not 13!), on row 16 you'll have 9 left, on row 17: 7 sts, and on row 18: 5 sts. FO and move on!

Crochet Edging

For the edging around the flaps, you need to hold 2 strands of **D** together at all times. If you don't, the Boston yarn will just swallow the bouclé up. All the flaps are edged exactly the same, so follow these instructions for all.

1. Insert your hook in very corner of flap—through both flap and hat—and pull the double strand of yarn through, ch 1, then sc 1 in each edge st (that's technically each row, since you're working vertically at the start) all around the flap.

2. Make last sc through both hat and flap again, sl st 1 somewhere along edge, and FO.

Attach Chin Ties

You want to fasten on the leather straps just as you would a fringe (see page 58), with 1 exception: don't fold the strap in half; instead, leave 1 side long (the side you'll tie) and the other side very short (just something to latch around so you can pull the strap through the crocheting). After you slip stitch 1 to fasten it, make a knot to hold it on good and tight.

I attached my ties between the flap and its crocheted edging, and I knotted each tie on the inside. If you like the look of the knot on the outside, though, or want it farther up the flap, don't let me stop you.

Fix That Funny Little Hole?

So this is what you get for knitting a hat bottom-up. A lot of people really dig the hole and just leave it the way it is. Others hate it, and, just in case you're one of those, let me tell you what they do: they turn the hat wrong side out, weave the **A** yarn in and out of each bind-off stitch at the edge of the hole, pull the yarn taut, and tie a knot.

I, on the other hand, dance along the happy middle ground: With hat RS out, hold 2 strands of **B** inside, and ch 1 through the 1st BO st, then sc 1 in every other BO st around. This closes the hole a little but not enough to make it pucker. Then sl st 1 through 1st ch at beg of rnd, and FO.

A note on hiding your tails: Hide all your tails on the cap part of the hat—even those left from the crocheted edging along the flaps. The only tails you won't be able to get into the hat will be the 1 strand left at the tip of each flap, and that strand you should tuck into the crocheted edging. The problem with the flap yarn is that it stitches up very tight and clean, which means it reveals all. Don't hide anything in it, because your flaps are just that: flappy. Your spectators will see even their underside now and then.

Block Garment

The flaps will flap much straighter and flatter if you iron them just a bit. See the instructions on page 25 if you don't know how.

Bow-Wow Cowl

I really dig cowls. They're like a hat and a scarf all in one, and you can take off one at any time and still keep the other. Letting the hood hang down is a fashion statement in itself, as well as ingeniously practical: it's beautiful *and* not lost! As for the Scotties on the sides, they're just plain classic.

ELEMENTS OF THIS DESIGN

knit	page 9
crochet	page 3
multistranding	page 51
turning corners	page 33
intarsia	page 44
buttonholes	page 55
picking up and building on	page 55
sewing	page 24

SIZE

hood width (at top): 10", length at back of head: 13", length along opening: 15"

collar width: 12", length: 2³/₄"

MATERIALS

Gedifra Fashion Trend (51% wool, 49% acrylic; 1.75 oz, 98 yds), colors **A** #4921—2 balls, and **C** #4904—1 ball

Schachenmayr nomotta Two in One (32% wool, 5% nylon, 63% acrylic; 1.75 oz, 87 yds), color **B** #04 bouclé sahara—1 ball

a bit of matching yarn or thread thin enough to sew on your buttons

2 buttons of your choice, maximum ²/₅" (about 10 mm) in diameter

5 mm and 8 mm knitting needles

2–3 mm and 5 mm crochet hook

sewing needle (size that fits your buttons)

You can attach more than 2 buttons if you'd like (read the pattern, and you'll understand your options).

GAUGE

St st and rib width: 5 sts=2", length: 3 rows=1"

Overview

You'll knit everything holding 2 strands together. The 1st piece will be the right side of the cowl (when you're wearing it), the 2nd will be the left. You knit each side in stockinette stitch from the top down, with an intarsia pattern worked into both sides. After you stitch the 2 sides together and crochet the edging, you'll pick up stitches to build on the ribbed, button-closed collar. To finish, you'll sew on the buttons.

Directions

Right Side

Base Row Holding 2 strands of **A** tog, CO 27 sts with the larger needles.

Rows 1–14 Work in St st, beg with k row. On every 2nd row, dec 1 by p tog 2nd and 3rd sts from end. In other words:

Row 1: K to end.

Row 2: P 24, p tog sts 25 and 26, p last st. (You now have only 26 sts.)

Row 3: K to end.

Row 4: P 23, p tog sts 24 and 25, p last st. (You now have 25 sts.) You get the idea, right?

After row 14, count to make sure you have dec to 20 sts.

Rows 15–22 Cont in St st, and also foll intarsia patt shown on page 84. For Scottie, work intarsia holding 2 strands of **B** tog. On row 22, count to make sure you have 20 sts. (If you have no experience with intarsia, first read the instructions on page 44. And don't believe what they tell you: it's easy—once you're into it.)

Rows 23–35 Still using (2 strands of) **A**, cont in St st for 13 rows.

BO in p.

Left Side

Base Row Holding 2 strands of **A** tog, CO 27 sts with the larger needles.

Rows 1–14 Work in St st, beg with k row. On every 2nd row, dec 1 by p tog the 2nd and 3rd sts (from beg, not end!). In other words:

Row 1: k to end.

Row 2: p 1, p tog 2nd and 3rd sts, p to end.

Rep patt for 14 rows total, and count to make sure you have dec to 20 sts on row 14.

I don't think you need an explanation for this, so I'm going to make it short: The decreases are made in the purl rows. When you work the right side of the cowl, the purl rows went from the front of the hood to the back. Now that you're working the left side, you're purling the hood from back to front. You want all the decreases to be on the same side of the hood (the back), so you have to do them at the beginning of your rows now that your rows begin at the back of the hood.

Rows 15–22 Cont in St st as you foll intarsia patt shown on page 85 (so that this pup faces forward, too). For the Scottie, work the intarsia holding 2 strands of **B** tog. On row 22, count to make sure you have 20 sts.

Rows 23–35 Still using (2 strands of) **A**, cont in St st for 13 rows.

BO in p.

Stitch Together

The external seam on this garment is much easier to do with a crochet hook than with a sewing needle, and I think it looks much cooler. You'll work with 2 strands of **C** so that the stitches are the same thickness as in the body of the cowl. That means you need to be careful not to make the stitches too tight,

INTARSIA FOR RIGHT SIDE OF COWL

ST #	1	2	3	4	5	6	7	8	9	10	11	12	13	14	15	16	17	18	19	20
→ Row 15							X		X				X							
← Row 16								X					X	X	X					
→ Row 17													X		X					
← Row 18								X					X	X						
→ Row 19									X	X	X	X	X							
← Row 20								X	X		X	X	X							
→ Row 21								X	X			X	X							
← Row 22								X		X		X		X	X					
ST #	20	19	18	17	16	15	14	13	12	11	10	9	8	7	6	5	4	3	2	1

because they should be the same size as all the other stitches. Just crochet them loosely, and check from time to time that they look about the same.

What's important is that the 2 pieces are sewn together matching and that the edges stay closed. If you miss a stitch (which is very likely to happen if you're not paying close attention, and who is?), don't freak out. Just make sure the edge is still straight and closed, and keep going. Now, when you come to the corner, really pay attention as you turn it, to make sure that those 3 stitches are all really in the same hole; otherwise that thing will pop right open the first time you get cold and pull the cowl tight.

1. Lay the 2 sides RS out, with WS tog (just as you would wear it). See how the shape is sort of a rec-tangle with a triangle jutting off 1 corner of it? Make sure point of triangle is on top and to your left, then line up the CO sts at top as accurately as possible. (Pinning them closed will help keep them in place.) The triangle's point will eventually jut off the back of your head—remember that as you crochet.

2. Insert larger crochet hook under 1st pair of CO sts at top right-hand corner of cowl (it's a right angle, not the triangle point). Make sure to go through both sides of cowl, or you won't be sewing anything tog. Pull (2 strands of) **C** through to the top, ch 1; insert hook under next pair of CO sts to left, and sc 1. Cont to sc 1 under each pair of sts until end of row (triangle point)—27 sc total.

INTARSIA FOR LEFT SIDE OF COWL

ST #	1	2	3	4	5	6	7	8	9	10	11	12	13	14	15	16	17	18	19	20
→ Row 15								X				X		X						
← Row 16						X	X	X					X							
→ Row 17						X		X												
← Row 18							X	X				X								
→ Row 19							X	X	X	X	X									
← Row 20							X	X	X		X	X								
→ Row 21							X	X			X	X								
← Row 22						X	X		X		X		X							
ST #	20	19	18	17	16	15	14	13	12	11	10	9	8	7	6	5	4	3	2	1

3. At triangle point, sc 2 more through the same 27th set of CO sts. (This gets you around the corner without puckering it up. See page 33 for more explanation.) Cont down back of cowl to the bottom, sc 1 in each pair of sts at end of each row—35 sc total. FO.

Crochet Edging

Now you're going to do the same thing around the hole that your lovely face will shine through. (Except that you obviously won't sew the 2 sides together here.) Still working with 2 strands of **C** and the smaller hook, lay the piece so that the triangle point is at the bottom left corner and the face hole is on top.

1. Insert larger hook just under 1st st at top right corner of upper piece only; ch 1, then sc 1 under each st until you reach top center.

2. Sc 1 through hole where you crocheted the pieces tog (you'll find room if you look hard enough), then cont to sc down other side of face hole to end—71 sc total. Ch 1 and FO.

Build On Collar

Place your work (right side out), with the only plain edge at the top and the triangle point at the left.

Decrease for Collar

To dec (which makes collar suck up a little tighter around your neck), use 2 strands of **C** and larger hook, as for rest of trimming. Insert hook under 1st BO st at top right corner of 1 layer only, ch 1; insert hook under next st to left, and sc 1.

Sc 1 under each of the foll BO sts, skipping each 10th st, until you reach center of cowl. Sc 1 through center st (where you crocheted 2 sides tog), and cont to sc to end, skipping each 10th st (cont counting from other side of center)—36 sc total.

Ch 10 (for flap), then FO.

Pick Up and Build On

The collar is ribbed so that it hugs your neck to keep it extra warm, but you're going to knit on a little extra flap, which you can button closed or leave open. (Ribbing the entire collar in a circle would give you wrinkles every time you pulled the cowl on and a facelift every time you pulled it off.) Obviously, this means you'll need buttonholes. You'll make them with a simple bind off/cast on technique that leaves a small hole between rows. Basically, you decrease 1 stitch in a row, and then add that stitch back on the next row to close up the hole. Let's get going, and you'll see what I mean.

1. Use the smaller needles and 2 strands of **B** tog to pick up all sts along bottom of cowl—the 1st ch, 36 sc, and 10 ch at end. (See page 55 if you don't know how to pick up stitches.)

2. Now you'll rib 10 rows, and work in buttonholes:

    Row 1: P 1, k 1, rep to end.

    Row 2: K the knits and p the purls.

    Row 3: P 1, k 1, p 1, then skp (that is, slip 4th st off onto right needle without knitting it, p 5th st as usual, and then use left needle to pass 4th st over

5th st and drop it off needle—just as you do when you BO); cont in rib (beg with k) to end of row.

Row 4: Rib 43 sts, CO 1 (just as you do at beg of a piece, with the fingerwork and all), then cont in rib (beg with p) to end of row.

Rows 5–6: K the knits and p the purls.

Rows 7–8: Rep rows 3–4.

Rows 9–10: K the knits and p the purls.

3. BO in rib, and use crochet hook to hide all tails.

Sew on Buttons

(Not much longer now.) Put on the cowl and close the collar by pulling the flap around your neck. Find the most comfortable position, and note where your buttonholes are. Mark the stitches on the flap where you want to sew the buttons (you can use pins or just hold your finger there). Use the sewing needle and a thinner yarn or thread to sew on the buttons.

It would be wise to sew on extra buttons at this point. Give yourself options: try the cowl on with a few of your winter garments to see if and where you want to add extra buttons.

Block Garment

The cowl doesn't really need to be blocked for the knitting. But you might want to block the intarsia a little to even out the stitches. And you do need to block the crochet to straighten out the edges. See page 25 on how to block using your iron.

Faux Fur Scarf

I use a special yarn to make this scarf, so that it gives the impression of fur. It also hides mistakes because of its irregular texture and bursts of fluffiness here and there. If you're a beginning knitter, this is the best place for you to start. It doesn't get any easier than this.

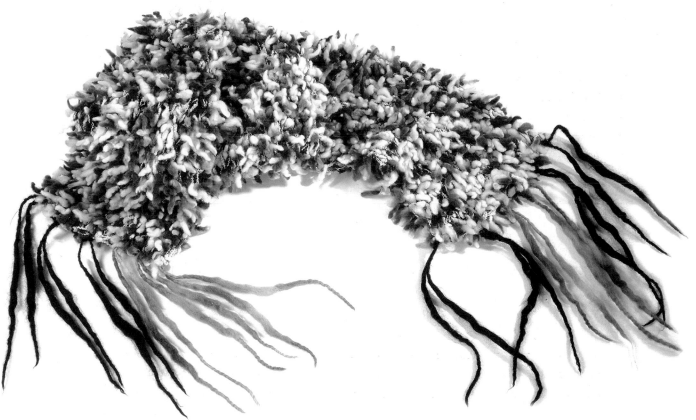

SIZE

width: 8", length: 70"

MATERIALS

Gedifra Carioca (92% wool, 8% nylon; 1.75 oz, 77 yds), color **A** #1816—6 balls

Gedifra Gigante (100% wool; 1.75 oz, 33 yds), color **B** #2332—1 ball

10 mm knitting needles

2–3 mm and 5 mm crochet hooks

GAUGE

It's just a scarf, people. The gauge really doesn't matter at all. If you find you don't make the 8" width, just knit more (or fewer) stitches. If you don't make the 70" length, just knit more (or fewer) rows.

Overview

You hold the yarn from 3 balls together and stitch stockinette all the way. It couldn't be easier—just let the yarn do the work. The 1 important thing: make sure to join all new yarn at the beginning of a row. When you see that you're down to about 3' on the 1st 3 balls, join new yarn at the beginning of the next row. Change all 3 together, even if 1 of the balls is still longer than 3' (it happens for some strange reason). When you knot together the ends of the old and new yarn at the end of the row, be careful to get all 6 strands into the knot. The knot should be tight, but don't let it tighten the loose, open stitch on the needle.

Directions

1. Line up ends of 3 strands of **A** so that fluffy tails are side by side (at least as much as possible). They're easier to work with this way.

2. Holding the 3 strands tog, and leaving about 3' of tail, CO 16 sts very loosely. It doesn't matter if the CO sts are different sizes; this yarn will hide all your "mistakes." Just be sure that all 3 strands of yarn make it onto needle with each st.

3. Work in St st until you run out of yarn—approx 140 rows. If you knit tightly, you'll have more rows; if you knit loosely, you'll have fewer.

4. Get ready to BO when you see that you have about 3' of yarn left. If you happen to be on a k row when you notice this, keep in mind that 3' is enough to do another p row and then BO.

Attach Fringes

Before you attach the fringes, choose a right side for the scarf, and use your smaller hook to hide the tails in the wrong side. (It might be kind of hard to tell which side is the right side. Technically, the knit side is, but if you can't tell the difference the peanut gallery won't be able to either.)

To make fringes, cut 10 pieces of **B** so that each piece has a thinner part of the yarn between 2 thicker parts at the ends. Make them double the length you want. To attach them, use your larger hook, and follow the instructions on page 58.

The Carioca yarn is pretty hard to work with, and it's hard to see the stitches when you're knitting 3 strands together. If working with it is beyond you (or if you just don't have the patience), use 4 balls of Schachenmayr nomotta Passion blau (45% wool, 45% acrylic, 10% nylon; 1.75 oz, 77 yds) for A instead. This will give you a scarf 63" long and 9" wide, but you need to make a few changes to the pattern:

1. Hold 2 (instead of 3) strands tog. (This scarf won't be as puffy.)

2. CO 18 (instead of 16) sts.

3. When you're done, edges will curl up nicely, but they don't feel nice, do they? To fix them use 3–4 mm crochet hook and A yarn to add a border that will weigh edges down: insert hook under 1st edge st, ch 1, sc 1 in each foll st all around edges—inserting your hook betw 1st and 2nd sts of each row on either side and under each CO/BO st on either end—and make sure you sc 3 in each corner to work your way around it gradually (see page 33 on turning corners in crocheting). At end, sl st 1 under ch at beg of round, and FO.

4. Iron crocheted border to flatten it out along edge. (See page 25 for instructions.)

Hey, you just got 2 completely different scarves out of one easy pattern. Good deal, right?

Keyhole Scarf

The advantage of the keyhole scarf is that you never need to knot it. You simply slip one end of the scarf through the keyhole and it will never blow or fall off. If you're a turtleneck fan, or your favorite coat has a collar that interferes with the knot of your scarf, crochet this real quick.

Overview

The scarf is crocheted mostly in a parallel net pattern, but with a keyhole inserted in the middle. You'll crochet external stripes on at the end, and then attach the fringes.

Directions

Base Row Using **A** and the larger hook, ch 36 to form the bottom row.

Row 1

1. Ch 5: 4 to build height, 1 to build width.

2. Tr 1 through 6th ch from hook.

3. *Ch 1, tr 1 through 2nd ch from hook; rep from * 17x—18 tr total.

Rows 2–30

1. Ch 5: 4 for height, 1 for width.

2. Tr 1 through the tr on the prev row (the st at the top of the tr, not the ch or space betw tr sts).

3. *Ch 1, tr 1; rep from * 17x—18 tr total.

Row 31: Making the Keyhole

1. Ch 1.

2. Sc 10 (1 betw tr, 1 through tr, 1 betw, etc.). Your last sc should be through the 6th tr.

3. Ch 15 (upward). (See photo on page 92, "Row 31: Making the Keyhole.")

4. Insert hook through 6th tr from end (see photo on page 92, "Row 31: Making the Keyhole"), and sc to end as in step 2: 11 sc.

Congratulations: you just made a keyhole. You have 1 chain stitch and 10 single crochets on one side of the

Row 31: Making the Keyhole

Row 32: Reinforcing the Keyhole

hole, the hole itself is 15 chains wide, and you have another 11 single crochets on the other side of it. It looks pretty symmetrical, right? That's because the width of 1 treble crochet equals the width of 1 single crochet and equals the width of 1 chain. Look at the row beneath the hole, and you'll find as well that 1 side has 6 treble crochets while the other has 5 trebles and 1 chain . . . yet the 2 sides are perfectly even.

Row 32: Reinforcing the Keyhole

1. Ch 1.

2. Sc 35—10 before the hole, 15 through the 15 ch sts themselves (see "Row 32: Reinforcing the Keyhole" above), and 11 after the hole.

Row 33

1. Ch 5: 4 to build height, 1 to build width.

2. Tr 1 through 6th sc from hook.

3. *Ch 1, tr 1 through 2nd ch from hook; rep from * 17x—18 tr total.

Rows 34–62

Crochet same as rows 2–30.

FO

Weave In External Stripes

Technically speaking, any kind of yarn you'd like to use for these "external stripes" will work, just as long as it's not thicker than the Boston yarn. (Using a thicker yarn will detract from the main yarn of the scarf. If you

Beginning a Stripe

Weaving In a Stripe

actually want the contrasting color to compete with the main color for attention, then go right ahead and use a yarn thicker than the Boston.) This is a great way to use up leftover yarn from other projects.

No matter what yarn you use, note this very important guideline: 1 chain here must equal 1 of the chain stitches you made between the treble crochets in the scarf. That's the distance between treble stitches in the scarf itself, and that's how loosely you need to crochet the chains of the stripes so that they don't bunch the treble stitches together.

Lay the scarf lengthwise in front of you, placing the right side (you choose one) facing up. You'll now work along the width of the scarf, not the length, and you'll alternate the Tecno Hair Lungo yarns, **B**, **C**, and **D** (unless you opted to use leftover yarn). There's no

prescribed number of stripes or alternating order. Just follow these instructions to crochet in the yarn any way you'd like.

1. Fold over **B** to make a tail about 4" long. Holding yarn above scarf, insert larger hook under side of the rectangle at edge of scarf, up through center of the rectangle, and through fold in the yarn; pull yarn under the column at the edge and up above garment (see photo above left), and ch 1 with both pieces of the folded yarn. (This fastens the yarn into place.)

2. With only the yarn (not the tail), ch 1 more, insert hook under parallel side of the rectangle, pull the yarn through to the top, then sl st 1 around this side of rectangle (see photo above).

Attach Fringes

Get ready by cutting 14 fringes from **E** (7 for each end of scarf). Make them double the length you want. Lay scarf RS up in front of you (it helps to do this on a hard, flat surface), and attach fringes according to instructions on page 58.

Don't pull the fringes through the stitches themselves; fasten them in the holes between treble stitches. Be sure to place them as evenly as possible along the edges: attach them 1st to the corners on each end, then in every 3rd rectangle from the ends, and put the last 1 in the middle, as evenly as you can between the 2 on either side of it (you can't space it perfectly).

3. *Ch 1 above garment; then insert hook under next tr, yo, pull through to above garment, and sl st 1; rep from * to end of row. Be careful not to insert your hook through tr sts themselves but only into holes of rectangles formed by them.

4. FO at end of each row. Hide all tails by using smaller hook to pull them through backs of "stripes": pull tail to back of garment, ch 1 through st nearest hook to fasten it into place, then simply pull through each of foll sts until tail is hidden.

Hippie Bikini Top

I got this idea from those colorful, happy, handmade bikinis of the 1960s. Let's face it, a knit bikini top does not work well for anyone larger than a B-cup. It's a small compensation for the less-endowed among us. If you're a C-cup, enlarge the cups at your own risk (of falling out of them in public). If you're a D, don't even think about wearing this.

SIZE

A-cup (B-cup)

width: 6" (6^1/$_2$–7")

length: 5^1/$_2$" (6")

MATERIALS

Gedifra Florida (50% cotton, 50% acrylic; 1.75 oz, 142 yds), 1 ball each of colors **A** #1420, **B** #1480, and **C** #1471

2 beads (with holes wide enough to pass through 2 strands of Florida yarn)

2–3 mm crochet hook

sewing needle/threader

GAUGE

width: 7 sc=1", length: 6 rows=1"

For this pattern you should definitely make a swatch and measure the tightness/looseness of your crochet. A few (seemingly tiny) 16ths-of-an-inch difference will make the (huge) difference between a bitchin' bikini and a potentially pornographic one. Check your gauge!

Overview

Even though your finished product is rather triangular, you're going to be crocheting more of a half-oval shape. As you read the instructions, pay close attention to the difference between "flip your work over," which means to flip it like a pancake, and "turn your work," which means to rotate it 180° so that the point of the oval that was on your right will now be on your left.

As for the bigger picture, it's clear and simple: knit 1 cup, knit the other, stitch on the straps and ties, hit the beach.

Directions

Base Row With A, ch 15 (18).

Row 1

1. Ch 1 (for height), then sc 1 in each st on base row—15 (18) sc total.

2. Ch 2, turn your work, then sc 15 (18) through same beginning 15 (18) ch from other side.

Let's be very clear on this: hold your work up in front of you vertically, like a column. You single-crocheted along the right side of the column already, so now you want to turn the corner around the top and continue to single-crochet down the left (see photo on page 97, "Direction of Crocheting Around Base Row"). Don't flip your work over and crochet on top of the

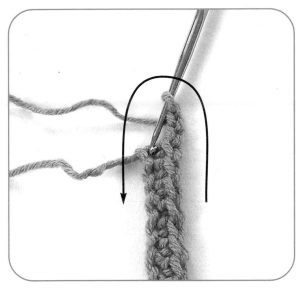

Direction of Crocheting Around Base Row

single crochets you already made. If you do this right, you'll see how you're crocheting an oval.

Row 2

1. OK: now flip your work over; ch 1, sc 15 (18), then sc 3 through hole under the 2 ch you made at top of oval on row 2.

2. Turn your work, and sc 15 (18) down other side of oval.

Here's how this works for the rest of the cup: between rows, *flip your work over* and begin crocheting up the "triangle" again. At the top of the triangle, *turn your work* to begin working your way down the other side.

Row 3

1. *Flip.* Join **B**, and ch 1, sc 16 (19), then sc 3 through very top st—the middle sc you made through hole at top of prev row; it's the 17th (20th) sc of prev row.

2. *Turn*, and sc 16 (19) down other side.

Row 4

1. *Flip.* Ch 1, sc 17 (20), sc 3 through very top st— 18th (21st) sc.

2 *Turn.* Sc 17 (20) down other side.

Row 5

1. *Ahem.* Join **C**, and ch 1, sc 18 (21), sc 3 through 19th (22nd) sc.

2. *Turn.* Sc 18 (21) down other side.

Row 6

1. *Flip.* Join **A**, and ch 1, sc 19 (22), sc 3 through 20th (23rd) sc.

2. *Turn.* Sc 19 (22) down other side.

Row 7

1. *Flip.* Ch 1, sc 20 (23), sc 3 through 21st (24th) sc.

2. *Turn.* Sc 20 (23) down other side.

Row 8

1. *Flip.* Join **C**, and ch 1, sc 21 (24), sc 3 through 22nd (25th) sc.

2. *Turn.* Sc 21 (24) down other side.

You probably have the pattern down by now. Let me just tell you why it is the way it is: the 1st chain of every row gives it height and connects it to the previous row; you're increasing 2 single crochets on every row (1 for each side of the "triangle") in order to accommodate both the width of the cup (which is expanding with each new row you add) and to build the height; the 3 single crochets at the top of each row both allow you to make the U-turn around the previous row (see "Turning Corners" on page 33 for more) and give the cup its outward-arching shape (which makes the room for your girlfriends).

Rows 9–15 Work patt, inc 2 at top of each row, and switching colors as follows:

> Rows 10–11: **B**
>
> Row 12: **A**
>
> Row 13: **C**
>
> Row 14: **B**
>
> Row 15: **C**. Row 15 is last row of patt for A-cup. Do not FO!

Rows 16–17 (for B-cup only) Cont with **C**, foll patt, but sc 32 on row 16 and 33 on row 17. (You probably didn't need to be told that, right?) This is last row of patt for B-cup. Do not FO!

Crochet Green Border

Now, for both sizes, you need to continue around the bottom of the cup to make a nice green border all the way around it. Obviously, you'll turn a corner, just as

you've done at the top of the "triangle" all along. Here's how to get around it without stretching your yarn or puckering up your cup:

1. Sc 2 more in the same (corner) st that you made the last sc in.

Now, as you crochet along the base, it's important to hold the cup facing up. How do you know which side is the right side? You've been cutting yarn off on what will be the back of the cup, so be sure that all the yarn you've cut until now is hanging below the garment.

There aren't really any stitches along the base for you to insert your hook in, but look closely and you'll see a little hole at the end of each row, just above the chains that join the rows together. These are the holes that you want to stitch through. Be careful not to skip a row.

2. Sc 27 (31) to the other end of the base.

3. Sc 2 more through the corner st.

4. Sl st 1 through 1st st around the corner, and FO.

Now's a good time to hide your tails. Knot 2 together wherever you can without distorting the shape of the cup. (Don't knot 3 together or you'll bunch up the rows.) Where you can't knot 2 together, just make a single crochet or a slip stitch with the single strand of yarn, and then hide it away. Hide all the tails underneath the green base of the triangle (otherwise they're likely to be seen).

Crochet Border: Windows

1. Hold cup RS up, with base of triangle at bottom. Insert your hook into bottom right corner stitch, from above, latch around **A**, pull the yarn to the top, ch 3, then hdc 1 under next green st (along side, not base—you're working border in same direction as you worked patt).

2. *Ch 2, hdc 1 under next green st; rep from * all around sides of cup until you reach left bottom corner—57x (67x) total.

Along the base of the triangle, you don't want the border to frill quite as much as on the sides. (Frilly won't stay put below your boob.) To keep the frilly look without so much yarn gyration, you'll simply decrease the number of stitches between the frills.

3. Ch 1, then hdc 1 under next green st; rep from * all across base until you reach the corner you began at—27x (31x) total.

4. At right bottom corner, ch 1, then sl st 1 through 3rd ch of prev row, and FO.

Obviously you need 2 of these cups, so go ahead and make another one. (I'll be patient.)

Crochet and Tie Straps

Now you need to designate a right and a left cup and stick with your decision, because you're about to put them together. Place both cups right side up and side by side; then cut 6 strands of **A**: two 6½' long and four 20' long. Fold each of them in half, because you're going to chain them into ties holding 2 strands together.

First you'll crochet the center straps that tie the 2 cups together.

1. Holding 1 of 6½' strands of **A** beneath 1 cup, insert your hook from above betw the green and orange yarns at the bottom corner that will sit in your cleavage; latch around fold in yarn, pull it through st, then sl st 1 through corner ch in orange yarn to fasten new yarn into place. (This is just like attaching a fringe.)

2. Ch 25, FO, pull on 1 of your beads (using a sewing needle or a threader will make this easier), and knot the yarn several times more to fasten it tight.

3. Rep steps 1–2 at bottom inside corner of other cup.

Now make the straps at the bottom outside corners of the base, which will tie around your back:

1. Holding 1 of the 20' strands of **A** beneath 1 cup, insert your hook from above betw green and orange yarns at corner, latch around fold in yarn, pull it through st, then sl st 1 through corner ch in orange yarn to fasten new yarn into place.

2. Ch 100, FO, and knot the yarn several times more to fasten it tight.

You're wondering if you can wear that Florida yarn into the water, aren't you? You can, technically. The yarn is a simple, sturdy cotton-acrylic blend, so water won't damage it. But you'll have to readjust the ties once you're in, because knits loosen up when wet, and a knit bikini won't hug your bosom as tightly as a manufactured one, so it's not ideal for serious swimming. Look at the picture of how this top fits, and you'll see what I mean. You'll probably want to reserve this one just for sunbathing and being seen.

3. Rep steps 1–2 at bottom outside corner of other cup.

Next, make straps at the top corner of each of the cups.

1. Rep step 1 of bottom outside ties, above.

2. Rep step 2 of bottom outside ties, but ch only 85–90.

3. Make 2nd neck strap same way.

4. Tie a knot near end of each center and neck strap. (These will help hold on next knots you'll tie.) Next, tie tog 2 straps joining cups, and then 2 neck straps. Make these knots relatively loose, try on bikini top, and adjust both knots so that it fits just right. Now make the knots (relatively) permanent. Then, every time you want to slip the bikini on, you need to tie only straps around your back.

Block Garment

You don't need to block or iron this, but if you want it to be softer, a gentle ironing will do the trick. See page 25 for instructions if you're not sure how to iron a knit.

Charleston Tank Top

Remember the flapper dress? Imagine it cut short at the waist (and knitted)—that's the look I was going for here. The punchy waist and light, open stitches make this top good for dancing, I think. The bright sunny colors are just to get you in the mood.

SIZE

S-M (L)

circumference around bottom: 28" (31"), length: 18" (20")

neckline width: 10" (11 1/2")

underarm length: 5 1/2"

MATERIALS

Gedifra Poesie (40% polyamide, 32% polyester, 28% microfaser; 1.75 oz, 98 yds), color **A** #2003—2 (3) balls

Gedifra Icaro (70% polyamide, 30% tactel; 1.75 oz, 82 yds), color **B** #1721—1 ball

Gedifra Florida (50% cotton, 50% acrylic; 1.75 oz, 142 yds), color **C** #1404—1 ball

4 leather strips, each 3 1/4' long

5 mm 32" circular knitting needle

5 mm straight knitting needles (optional)

2–3 mm crochet hook

stitch holder/huge safety pin/extra yarn

stitch marker/extra yarn (whatever you use to remind you where rounds begin)

GAUGE

width: 7 sts=2", length: 2 extended rows=2"

Overview

Very simple: you knit everything in the round from the bottom, with extended stitches, decreasing to shape the underarms and neckline when the time comes. Add a crochet edging to the top and bottom, then weave in the shoulder and waist straps, and you're all done.

Directions

Base Rnd With the circular needle and **A**, CO 100 (110) sts. Join in a ring, making sure you haven't twisted the sts on the needle.

Rnd 1 K all sts.

Here's how this works for a while: you want to make extended stitches, which means that on 1 round you yarn over between your knit stitches, and on the next you unravel that yarned over yarn (for more explanation and photos, see page 49). You knit all the stitches on round 1 without yarning over because you need a good, sturdy base row. From then on, though, you follow this pattern:

Even rnds K all sts, yo 1 in betw each st.

Odd rnds K all sts, unraveling the yo yarn from prev row as you go. Remember to stretch your piece at end of each row to even the extended sts.

For colors, follow this list. Pay attention to where you can drag along the yarn and where you need to cut:

> Rnds 2–5: **A**
> Rnd 6: **B**
> Rnds 7–9: **A**
> Rnd 10: **B**
> Rnds 11–31 (11–35): **A**

OK. Next you'll do the underarms, working the front and back of the tank top separately.

Front of Underarms

1. Move 1st 50 (55) sts onto a holder, but leave last 50 (55) on your needle (or put them onto straight needles, if you prefer to do this as a flat piece).

2. Turn work to other side (p side, which actually will be RS).

Row 32 (36) Cont in **A**, BO 4 sts, then p 46 (51) to end. The BO (dec) sts are at the underarms, and as you go you'll see that you don't want extended stitches there, because you need strong, closed stitches for finishing.

Row 33 (37)

1. BO 4 sts to dec.

2. *K 1, yo 1; rep from * until next-to-last st—42x (47x) total.

3. Simply k 2. (Again, you don't want an extended stitch here because it would leave a big hole that you couldn't crochet through later.)

Row 34 (38) BO 1, unravel yo yarn from prev row (*don't BO or p with this yarn!*), BO 1, unravel next yo yarn, BO 1, then p rest of sts to end, unraveling as you go—39 (44) p total.

Row 35 (39) K just like row 33, but BO only 3 at beg—36 (41) k total.

Row 36 (40) BO 1, unravel yo yarn, BO 1, then p to end, unraveling as you go—34 (39) p total.

Row 37 (41) K just like row 33, but BO only 2 at beg—32 (37) k total.

Row 38 (42) BO 1, unravel yarn, then p to end, unraveling as you go—31 (36) p total.

Row 39 (43) K just like row 33, but BO only 1 at beg—30 (35) k total.

Rows 40–44 (44–48) You've done the underarms for now, so just cont making extended sts: unravel and p on each even row, and yo and k on each odd row. On row 41 (45), join and k with **B**, but cut it at the end of the row, and cont with **A** to the end.

Row 45 (49) K all sts, without yo.

BO in p.

Back of Underarms

1. To shape underarms on back, lay garment RS out with unfinished side (back) facing up. Insert your needle *from left to right* through the 50 (55) stitches on holder.

2. Foll directions for front of underarms, rows 32 (36) through BO exactly. At end, cut all your yarn, tie ends, and hide tails.

Crochet Edging: Windows

To crochet on the edging around the top and bottom of the garment, you'll use the **C** yarn. Keep the garment right side out as you work.

Bottom

Begin where you began all your knitting, on either the left or the right side (it's where the tails were hanging).

1. Insert your hook under 1st CO st, ch 2, and hdc 1 under next CO st.

2. *Ch 1, hdc 1 under next CO st; rep from * all around—99x (109x) total.

3. Sl st 1 through 2nd ch at beg of rnd, and FO.

Top

You'll follow the same instructions here as for the bottom edging, but obviously these aren't cast-on stitches. Begin at the bottom of an underarm, ideally on the side where you began all your knitting. As you work the pattern in each stitch along the edge, you'll see there's some room for error. You want to chain and half double crochet *under each bind-off stitch*. Along the top, the bind off stitches are pretty clear-cut, but along the underarms, you have to make sure to chain and half-double-crochet under each BO stitch that you made as a decrease, *not* just once in each row (there's a difference there—have a look).

All in all, you'll have about 45 half double crochets in each underarm and exactly 30 (35) along each top edge. As long as the crocheting in the underarms doesn't stretch or crimp up any of your stitches, it's OK if you miss or duplicate 1 here and there. Just pay attention as you work, and pause now and then to make sure the edging looks all right. Don't forget to slip stitch through the 2nd chain when you get back to where you started, just as you did on the bottom edging.

Weave In Shoulder Straps and Waist Tie

Here's the whole point of all that crocheting (besides the fact that it's just gorgeous, of course): you want to weave the leather strips (2 for the shoulder straps, 2 along the waist) through the holes in the crocheting. Use the hook to help pull them through, and see page 59 for more explanation if you've never done this before.

At the shoulders, make sure to insert the strips at the very top corner of the knitting. Tie bows at the top once you've got them in. When you do the bottom, first lay the tank top on a flat surface and make 2 nice creases along the sides. Insert the leather strips right at those side folds.

Classic Sleeveless Sweater

The only thing imaginative about this sweater is the yarn I use to make it. Otherwise it's as classic as the little black dress. If you don't have one of these yet, get your favorite color yarn and make one now. It's a must in every wardrobe.

SIZE

S-M (L)

body circumference: 35" (38–39"),
length: 21 1/2"

turtleneck circumference: 20", length: 4"

waistband circumference: 34" (38"),
length: 2"

armholes length: 8"

MATERIALS

Schachenmayr nomotta Passion (45% wool,
45% acrylic, 10% nylon; 1.75 oz, 77 yds),
color **A** #83 Mexiko—6 balls

Schachenmayr nomotta Hair (65% mohair,
35% acrylic; 1.75 oz, 208 yds), color **B** #32
kirsch—1 ball

Schachenmayr nomotta Boston (70% acrylic,
30% wool; 1.75 oz, 60 yds), color **C** #32
burgund—1 ball

8 mm straight knitting needles

8 mm, 32" circular knitting needle

2–3 mm and 5 mm crochet hooks

cable needle

stitch markers/extra yarn (whatever you use
to remind you where rounds begin)

stitch holder/big safety pin/extra yarn
(whatever you prefer for holding stitches)

safety/straight pins

GAUGE

Rib & St st width: 5 sts=2",
length: 3 rows=1"

Overview

The sweater is worked in 2 pieces, 1st the front, then
the back. On both you knit from the bottom up,
beginning with the ribbed waist and switching to
stockinette stitch for the body.

The cables on the front are each 9 rows high,
which means that you twist them on each 10th row.
Since the purl side is the right side of the garment,
the cables are always twisted when purling. Don't
forget to pick up **B** *together with* **A** when you begin
knitting the cables. The rest of the body is done with
A alone. (I added the contrasting color to the design

because the extra yarn makes the cable a little puffier and the color makes the cable more vivid. **B** is much thinner than **A**, though, and if you have enough to worry about just doing a cable, and you find the added yarn too hard to work with, just leave it out.)

You stitch the 2 pieces together, crochet around the armholes, decrease the neckline in crochet, and then pick up the crochet stitches to knit the turtleneck. At the end I'll give you instructions on how to block this garment, since it's so special.

Directions

Front

Base Row With straight needles and **A**, CO 43 (47) sts.

Rows 1–5 Rib all sts, beg with p 1, k 1.

You just created a ribbed waist. Now you'll work the rest of the front in stockinette stitch. You have to begin creating the cables, though, so here's the idea: on either side of the cables are 14 (16) stitches, the cables are 6 stitches each, and 3 stitches are between them. Have a look at the next few rows, and see if you can figure out the logic behind them.

Rows 6–9 Work all rows in St st, joining **B** *tog with* **A** for cables (and the 3 sts betw them), and dropping it again on other side. (Don't cut **B**. You'll use it all up on front of sweater. Simply pick it up and drop it again on each row.) Just so you feel nice and secure, I'll hold your hand this time:

Row 6: P 14 (16), join **B** *tog with* **A** and k 6, p 3, k 6, drop **B**, p 14 (16).

Row 7: K 14 (16), pick up **B** *tog with* **A** and p 6, k 3, p 6, drop **B**, k 14 (16).

Row 8: Rep row 6.

Row 9: Rep row 7.

Before you go diving into this, you might want to review the instructions (with photos) for cables on page 47. I give tips there for getting the best cable possible. Go on, review it. (I'm serious.)

Row 10

1. P 14 (16).

2. Slip next 3 sts onto cable needle, and move it to *back* of your work. Holding cable needle *behind your work* (this is super important), *pick up B tog with A* and k next 3 sts that are on your left needle. Bring cable needle back to front of your work. (At this point, you can also place sts from cable needle back on your left needle, but make sure you put them on so that *1st st on is last st you took off.*) K 3 sts from cable needle *in order*, that is, don't twist them or k the left st 1st.

3. P 3.

4. Rep step 2 to twist 2nd cable, but hold cable needle *in front* of your work. (This makes cable twist the other way.)

5. Now drop **B**, and with just **A**, p 14 (16) to end.

Rows 11–19 Work just like rows 6–9 (picking up **B** where necessary).

Row 20 Work just like row 10 to twist your cables.

Rows 21–29 Work just like rows 11–19.

Row 30 Work like row 10.

Rows 31–39 Work like rows 11–19.

Row 40 Work like row 10.

Rows 41–49 Work like rows 11–19.

Row 50 Work like row 10.

Now you'll start decreasing for the armholes by binding off stitches at the beginning of each row. Otherwise, though, the pattern continues exactly the same. (Don't forget to keep picking up **B**!)

Row 51 BO (in k) 2 sts, then k 11 (13), p 6, k 3, p 6, and k 14 (16).

Row 52 BO (in p) 2 sts, then p 11 (13), k 6, p 3, k 6, and p 12 (14).

Take a moment to notice what you've done: you decreased at the beginning of the row, worked the middle section with the cables as usual, and decreased 2 stitches at the other end at the beginning of the next row. You'll continue decreasing this way, always keeping the middle with the cables normal.

Row 53 BO (in k) 1 st, then k 10 (12), work the middle (p 6, k 3, p 6), and k 12 (14) to end.

Row 54 BO (in p) 1 st, p 10 (12), work the middle (k 6, p 3, k 6), and p 11 (13) to end.

Row 55 BO 1 st, k 9 (11), work the middle, k 11 (13) to end.

Row 56 BO 1 st, p 9 (11), work the middle, p 10 (12) to end.

Row 57 BO 1 st, k 8 (10), work the middle, k 10 (12) to end.

Row 58 BO 1 st, p 8 (10), work the middle, p 9 (11) to end.

Row 59 Don't BO! Just k 9 (11), work the middle, and k 9 (11) to end.

Row 60 Now cont in St st without dec, but twist your cables as you did in row 10.

Rows 61–69 Cont in St st with cables, without dec, picking up **B** where necessary.

Row 70 Cont in St st, twisting your cables in the middle.

Rows 71–72 Cont in St st, picking up **B** where necessary.

All right. You're done with **B**, so you can cut it and put it away. Get out your stitch holder (or whatever you prefer to use), and pay some serious attention. I didn't understand what I was doing with shoulders for years, and most people I know just follow the pattern without trying to understand. I'm going to take my time explaining the logic to you so that you can design your own garments in the future—listen up and look closely.

Right Shoulder

Row 73 K 9 (11), BO 15 with just **A** (this is the whole middle section—yes, you're done cabling!), cut the yarn, and put the last 9 (11) sts of this row onto your holder.

The stitches you knit are going to be the right shoulder; those last 9 (11) stitches are the left shoulder. You're going to finish the right one 1st, then go back and do the left. You'll do them differently, though, and this is what I want you to pay attention to.

Row 74 Join new yarn (**A**), BO (in p) 1 st in order to dec it, and p 7 (9) to the end. What you just did was decrease along the curve in the neckline, making room for your head.

Row 75 K all sts to cont in St st.

Row 76 BO (in p) 1 st to dec, then p 6 (8) to end.

BO all rem sts on the right shoulder.

Left Shoulder

Now place all the stitches on your holder back onto your needle, starting with the stitches toward the middle of the garment (where your cables are). (Why from the middle to the outside? You're decreasing at the neckline, so you need to start from the arm edge on row 73 in order to be at the neck edge when you start row 74, to match the right shoulder.) Inserting the needle from the middle to the outside means you'll have to begin row 73 with the right side facing you, so it'll be a purl row, not a knit row, like it was for the right shoulder.

Row 73 Join **A** and p 9 (11) to end of row.

Row 74 Flip your work, and voilà! You're at the neckline where you can decrease. Simply BO (in k) 1 st in order to dec it, then k 7 (9) to end.

Row 75 P all sts to cont in St st.

Row 76 BO (in k) 1 st to dec, then k 6 (8) to end.

BO all rem sts.

Back

It's all downhill from here. You'll be done in no time.

Base Row With your straight needles and **A**, CO 43 (47) sts.

Rows 1–5 Rib all sts, beg with k 1, p 1.

Rows 6–50 Work all rows in St st, beg with p row.

Row 51 BO (in k) 2 sts, and k 40 (44) to end.

Row 52 BO (in p) 2 sts, and p 38 (42) to end.

Row 53 BO (in k) 1 st, and k 37 (41) to end.

Row 54 BO (in p) 1 st, and p 36 (40) to end.

Row 55 BO 1, and k 35 (39).

Row 56 BO 1, and p 34 (38).

Row 57 BO 1, and k 33 (37).

Row 58 BO 1, and p 32 (36).

Rows 59–74 Cont in St st without dec.

Left Shoulder

Here are the shoulders again, so you've got another chance to get this, in case you didn't catch on before. If you got it, great; reinforce your knowledge by not looking at the pattern!

Row 75 K 9 (11), BO 15, then cut yarn, and place last 9 (11) sts on your holder.

Row 76 Using 1st 9 (11) sts that you left on your needles, join new yarn (**A**), BO 2 sts to dec them, then p 6 (8) to end of row.

BO all rem sts on the left shoulder.

Right Shoulder

Row 75 Transfer all sts on your holder to your needle, starting from middle of garment (where you have the 15 BO sts) and going to outside; then p 9 (11) across the row.

Row 76 BO 2 sts to dec, and k 6 (8) to end of row.

BO all rem sts.

Stitch Together

Lay the 2 pieces 1 on top of the other, with wrong sides out and right sides touching. Line up their edges as neatly as possible, and pin them together along the edge stitches.

1. Holding **A**, insert smaller crochet hook into 2nd st in from edge at bottom of 1 underarm and through same st on same row in other piece; pull yarn through, and sl st 1.

2. Sl st 1—always in 2nd pair of sts in from edge—all the way down to CO rows, then FO.

3. Rep to stitch up other side.

4. Rep at shoulders, but go through each pair of BO sts (yes, BO sts themselves, on the very edge).

Crochet Edging

Now turn the garment right side out, and lay it so that you can work comfortably around 1 of the armholes. You'll need **C** and the larger crochet hook for the edging.

1. Beg at seam at bottom of armhole. Insert your hook betw sts 1 and 2, yo, pull yarn through, and ch 1.

2. Sc 1 in each foll st all the way around armhole.

3. Sl st 1 through ch at beg of rnd, and FO.

Do the same on the other armhole. That's it.

Build On Turtleneck

Lay the sweater front side up (and RS out) with the neck hole to your right. You'll need **C**, the larger crochet hook, and the circular needle to complete the project. You'll skip stitches to decrease the hole, and you need to scatter them among the sections of the sweater. I'll give you directions by section; be sure to space your skipped stitches evenly in each section. Take the time to count your stitches as you work from landmark to landmark. You always insert your hook between the 1st and 2nd stitches on the edge.

Decrease Neckline

1. In left shoulder, insert your hook into the st that you sewed through, pull **C** through st, ch 1, and sc 5 (evenly spaced) to beg of 1st cable.

2. Sc 15 under the BO sts to end of 2nd cable.

3. Sc 6 to seam on right shoulder.

4. Sc 4 to beg of BO row on back.

5. Sc 15 under BO sts along back.

6. Sc 4 back to left shoulder seam.

7. Sl st 1 through the 1st ch, FO, and knot tails.

Picking Up and Building On

1. With circular needle, pick up (through the back!) all sts that you just crocheted around neck (see page 55 for instructions). Make sure you have 50.

2. Rib 10 rnds, starting with k 1, p 1.

3. BO in rib, hide all your tails, and then read about blocking this garment so that all your hard work doesn't go up in flames.

Block Garment

The yarn you used for this sweater has wool and mohair in it, so you need to be extra careful when you block it. First of all, you need to iron only the sewing along the sides and shoulders, so leave the rest of the sweater alone. Secondly, even though you might use medium-low or even medium heat on other garments, use only low on this one. Make sure that the cloth between the iron and the sweater stays damp, and *don't* rub the iron back and forth: place it gently on one spot, and, the second you see steam, pick it up, and place it gently on the next. Press very lightly—*don't rub!* Do it right, and you'll be enjoying your sweater's warm embrace for years to come.

Forest Witch Shawl

In my imagination, the candy-house-dwelling, little-kid-eating witch from "Hansel and Gretel" wears a shawl like this. Obviously hers is older and more raggedy, though, so I had to make yours a little more fashionable and feminine. If you plan to eat children in this, you might want to leave off the friendly happy flower.

ELEMENTS OF THIS DESIGN

crochet	page 3
staggered net	page 35
multistranding	page 51
fringes	page 58
sewing	page 24

SIZE

width: 57", length: 35–36"

MATERIALS

Gedifra Fashion Trend Stripe (51% wool, 49% acrylic; 1.75 oz, 98 yds), color **A** #4669—3 balls

Gedifra Byzanz (60% acrylic, 20% wool, 15% polyamide, 5% polyester; 1.75 oz, 33 yds), color **B** #1669—1 ball

Schachenmayr nomotta Two in One (32% wool, 5% nylon, 63% acrylic; 1.75 oz, 87 yds), colors **C** #08 bouclé herbstzauber— 1 ball, and **D** #06 bouclé steppe—1 ball (divide **D** into 2 balls)

matching thread (shades of green are best)

2–3 mm and 5 mm crochet hooks

safety/straight pins

sewing needle

GAUGE

The size of the rectangles doesn't matter, so neither does the size of the stitches. You just want to make sure that the shawl measures at least 57" wide, unless you prefer it to be narrower. If you want it wider, increase the base only in increments of 10 chain stitches. (This keeps the angles of the triangle nice and straight as you decrease.)

Overview

The shawl is crocheted in a triangular shape, from base to tip, using the net pattern introduced on page 34. Decreases are made at the beginning of each row by slip stitching to the center of the 1st rectangle on the previous row, and at the end of each row by fastening the last stitch in the center of the last rectangle on the previous row. In other words, half a rectangle is decreased on either side on every row. To finish, you make and sew on the flower, and add the fringes.

Directions

Base Row With larger hook and **A**, ch 180 sts.

Row 1 Ch 1 for height, then sc 180 to end.

Row 2

1. Ch 7 (2 for height, 5 for length), then dc 1 in 5th st of prev row.

2. *Ch 5 for length and dc 1 in 5th st of prev row; rep from * to end—35x total.

Row 3

1. Sl st 3 to reach center of 1st rectangle on the prev row (this is how you dec), ch 2 for height and 5 for length, then hdc 1 in center of next rectangle.

2. *Ch 5, hdc 1 in center of next rectangle; rep from * to end—34x total. (Last hdc should be through center ch in last rectangle of prev row. This is how you dec at end of each row.)

Rows 4–36 Work same as row 3, dec 1 on each row (it happens automatically if you just foll the directions) until only 2 rectangles are left on row 36.

Row 37 Sl st 3, ch 7, dc 1 in 3rd st from column, and ch 1.

FO

Crochet and Sew on Flower

Center

1. With **C** and larger hook, ch 10; sl st 1 through 1st ch to connect the sts into a circle.

2. Ch 1 for height, then sc 18 through the center of the circle—not through ch sts themselves; sl st 1 through the 1st sc.

Petals

3. *Ch 12, then sl st 1 through 2nd sc on prev row; rep from * around the flower for a total of 9 petals.

Now you'll work from inside each petal to buff up its borders.

4. *Sc 18 through center—not sts themselves—of 1st petal you made, and sl st 1 through same sc that you sl st through in step 3; rep from * 9x total to thicken outline of each petal, then FO.

Stem

In 1 hand, hold both flower (RS up) and 2 strands of **D** tog. Insert larger hook from above into 1 hole betw 2 petals and center of flower; pull yarn through hole, sl st 1 to fasten it into place, then ch 120. FO.

Sewing

Place the flower as you like it on the shawl (I like it with the flower's center just between my shoulder blades and the stem running over my shoulder), and fasten it down with safety or straight pins (see photo on page 116, "Fastening Down the Flower"). With the sewing needle and matching thread, sew the flower on from the wrong side of the shawl.

Here are your guidelines:

1. Don't stretch anything! Don't force shawl out of shape or warp form of petals just to tie them down. (Many of us could use this advice as well in

Fastening Down the Flower

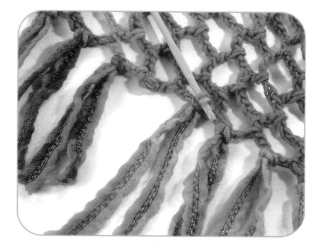

Spacing the Fringes

our love lives.) Don't pull yarn or thread. Just stitch everything where it naturally falls.

2. Sew each petal top once or twice (however many times you can get it done without stretching it) to junction of 2 rectangles.

3. Sew on stem about every 2", making leaves as you go.

4. Leaves are simply loops you make in stem; sew them on only at tip and base, not sides. At base of each leaf, make sure that you sew through both pieces of stem that overlap each other to form loop.

Why'd I give in and sew? If you've already made Pippi's Fishnet Skirt (page 138), you saw the insanity required to crochet on the flower. It was to spare you, my fellow knitters, that I picked up that wretched sewing needle. All for you.

Now, are you ready to cut up the yarn you paid half a week's salary for? Let's go.

Attach Fringes

Cut 76 strings of **B**, each about 10" long. You'll use the larger hook to attach the fringes just like any other fringes (see page 58 for instructions). Remember always to work on the same side of your garment when adding fringes. Now, here's *where* to add them:

1. At top (shoulder edge) of shawl, attach your corner fringes by pulling 1 fringe through very 1st st in base row and another through very last st.

2. Down both sides, pull each fringe through 2nd st from base of each rectangle, as in the photo on page 116, "Spacing the Fringes." (Where you have a ch on 1 edge, you'll have a hdc on the other, because you flipped garment at each row and you start each row with ch sts.)

3. On bottom rectangle (last row), pull 1 fringe through each of its bottom corners.

Rich Gypsy Cape

Since there's no such thing as a rich gypsy, you've probably guessed that this garment is a hybrid. The cut is from the cape traditionally worn by European aristocracy, but the combination of black and gold and a burst of color is typically gypsy. This is a great piece to wear when it's just a little chilly and you don't want to have to hold onto a shawl.

Overview

You knit all rounds on a circular needle in an extended stitch pattern, with 1 row of regular stitches between each pair of rows that forms the extended stitches. The body is knit from the bottom up, with decreases spaced throughout. You crochet the neck on; then you add a "stripe" at the bottom of the neck area and a crocheted edging around the bottom.

Always let the yarn hang outside the circle formed by the circular needle, join new yarn at the beginning of a round, and mark the beginning of each round if you can't tell it otherwise.

Directions

Base Rnd With A, CO 140 sts.

Rnd 1 K all sts.

Rnd 2: Extended Stitches K 1, *yo twice, k 1; rep from * to end of rnd. (If you don't understand this or are tempted to do something with those yo loops, turn to page 49, and read carefully.)

Rnd 3: Extended Stitches K all sts, unwrapping double loops that you yo on prev rnd betw each st. Stretch your work to extend sts.

Rnd 4 K all sts.

Rnds 5–6 Rep rnds 2–3.

Rnd 7 K all sts, dec each 14th st (that is, k 12, k 13 and 14 tog, k 12 more, k 2 tog, and so on). You'll make 10 total dec and have 130 sts rem at end of rnd. Count them!

Rnds 8–9 Rep rnds 2–3.

Rnd 10 K all sts.

Rnds 11–12 Rep rnds 2–3.

Rnd 13 K all sts, dec each 13th st (that is, k 11, k 12 and 13 tog, k 11 more, k 2 tog, and so on.) You'll make 10 total dec and have 120 sts rem at end of rnd. Count to be sure.

Rnds 14–15 Rep rnds 2–3, then cut **A**.

Rnd 16 Join **B**, and k all sts, dec each 12th st (k 10, k 2 tog, to end of rnd). You'll dec 10 sts and have 110 sts rem.

Rnds 17–18 Rep rnds 2–3 (but with **B**), then cut **B**.

Rnd 19 Join **A**, and k all sts, dec every 11th st (k 9, k 2 tog to end). You'll dec 10 and have 100 sts.

Rnds 20–21 Rep rnds 2–3.

Rnd 22 K all sts, dec every 10th st (k8, k 2 tog).

Rnds 23–24 Rep rnds 2–3.

Rnd 25 K all sts, dec every 9th st. You'll have 80 sts.

Rnds 26–27 Rep rnds 2–3.

BO

Before you even pick up your crochet hook, turn your work right side (that's purl side) out, and find the tails, which should all be hanging in a line (if you joined all your yarn at the beginning of the rounds, as I recommended). That's where you started your rounds, so that's where you want to start crocheting all of the stuff you're about to add on.

Crochet Neck

This is going to be a breeze. Whip out your larger hook and the **D** yarn.

1. Insert hook under 1st BO st, *ch 1, then sc 1 in 2nd st from hook; rep from * all around—39 sc total + 1 ch; sl st 1 under 1st ch.

2. On next row, ch 2, then dc 1 through each sc all around—39 dc total + 2 ch; sl st 1 in 2nd ch at beg.

3. On 3rd row, ch 2, then dc 1 in 1st 3 dc on prev rnd; then * skip 1 st, dc 1 in next 4, skip 1, dc 4, all around—31 dc total + 2 ch; sl st 1 in 2nd ch at beg, and FO.

If you want your neck a little higher, you can add a 4th row, just like the 3rd, but don't skip any stitches, because the 31 double crochets make the opening tight enough.

Crochet Neck Bottom and Cape Bottom Edgings: Shells

This edging is a simple "stripe" formed by the shell pattern (that's a fundamental design I explained on page 38). If you've done shells before, the edgings will go even faster than the neck. If you haven't, take a look at page 38 and practice a little; then come back here to see where to put the shells on your cape.

Look closely at the 1st row of single crochet stitches at the neck of the cape. (It's the row where you joined the **D** yarn to the bound-off **A** yarn stitches.) Poke around under that row a little, and you'll see how the black yarn is strung through each single crochet. As you add on the shells, make sure to insert your hook through each single crochet stitch itself and under the black yarn that it's attached to (see photo, "Crocheting shells onto the bound-off stitches"). You're actually attaching the shells to the black bound-off stitches; you just have to get to them by going through the single crochets you've already stuck on them. Fastening the shells to the black just makes them hold on that much tighter; were you to attach them to the single crochet stitches only, the shells would pull those stitches forward, making them look limp, eventually stretching them out of shape, and even tearing them.

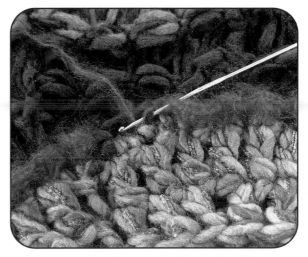

Crocheting shells onto the bound-off stitches

1. Holding **C**, insert your smaller hook through 1st sc and under the black yarn it's attached to; then ch 3, dc 1, ch 2, and dc 1—all under the same st.

2. *Insert hook through next sc and under black yarn; dc 1, ch 2, dc 1—all under same st; rep from * to end of rnd—39 shells total.

3. Sl st 1 through 3rd ch of 1st shell, and FO.

Now place bottom edge of cape on top so that you can work comfortably along it. Follow same directions to add shell edging to CO row, making 1 shell under each 2nd CO stitch—69 shells total.

Lara's Muff

OK, so Lara's muff didn't have puppy dogs on it in the original *Dr. Zhivago*, but I did get the idea from the movie. A muff out-does mittens and gloves in lots of situations. It's the easiest way to keep your digits warm when you just want to get from your house to the heated car. It's the most elegant thing when you're gliding across an icy lake. And, of course, it's one of the best places to hide a gun. You can also double up by wearing mittens and a muff.

SIZE

body width: 10", length: 6$^1/_2$"

cuffs width: 1$^1/_2$", length: 5"

MATERIALS

Gedifra Fashion Trend (51% wool, 49% acrylic; 1.75 oz, 98 yds), colors **A** #4962—2 balls, and **C** #4925—1 ball

Schachenmayr nomotta Two in One (32% wool, 5% nylon, 63% acrylic; 1.75 oz, 87 yds), color **B** #90 bouclé marmor—1 ball

2 buttons of your choice, maximum $^4/_5$" (about 20 mm) in diameter

4 leather strips, each 3$^1/_4$'

5 mm and 8 mm knitting needles

2–3 mm and 5 mm crochet hooks

sewing needle (size that fits your buttons)

GAUGE

stockinette stitch width: 5 sts=2", length: 3 rows=1"

rib width: 2 sts=1", length: 3 rows=1"

Overview

You knit the body of the muff from the top of the front side straight through to the top of the back, working in stockinette stitch from beginning to end. The intarsia for the Scottie dogs is given in chart Z. After you decrease in crochet for the hand holes, you build on the cuffs in rib and stitch the piece together with a visible crochet seam along the top. There are no buttonholes: you just sew the buttons onto an extra flap of ribbing to give the look of fastened cuffs.

Directions

Front

Base Row With larger needles and holding 2 strands of **A** tog, CO 25 sts.

Rows 1–6 Work in St st, beg with a k row.

Rows 7–14 Cont in St st, and foll intarsia patt shown on page 124. (Turn the book upside down if that makes it easier to foll patt, since that's the way you're knitting it.) For Scotties, work intarsia holding 2 strands of **B** tog. (You've never knit intarsia before? Check out the explanation on page 44, and you'll have your puppies in no time.) At end, drop **B**.

Rows 15–21 Still using (2 strands of) **A**, cont in St st for 7 rows.

INTARSIA FOR MUFF

ST #	1	2	3	4	5	6	7	8	9	10	11	12	13	14	15	16	17	18	19	20	21	22	23	24	25
→ Row 7				X		X				X						X				X		X			
← Row 8				X						X	X	X		X	X	X					X				
→ Row 9										X		X		X		X									
← Row 10						X				X	X			X	X				X						
→ Row 11							X	X	X	X	X			X	X	X	X	X							
← Row 12						X	X			X	X	X		X	X	X			X	X					
→ Row 13						X	X			X	X			X	X				X	X					
← Row 14				X		X		X		X	X			X	X		X		X		X				
ST#	25	24	23	22	21	20	19	18	17	16	15	14	13	12	11	10	9	8	7	6	5	4	3	2	1

Back

You knit the back the same as the front, only without the Scotties. (If you're a symmetry freak, go ahead and knit intarsia again. Just make sure to flip dogs top to bottom.)

Rows 22–42 Cont in St st for 21 rows.

BO in k.

Build On Cuffs

You make the cuffs in rib so that they create a sort of vacuum suck around your wrists. You'll build them onto the sides of the muff, giving them a little extra tab to "button closed" later, so that they resemble shirt cuffs.

Decrease Holes

You don't want the holes for your hands to be as big as the piece is long right now, so you'll reduce the number of stitches around each edge.

1. Lay piece flat, RS up, with Scotties standing on their heads at bottom. Then turn piece clockwise 90°, so that you can work along left length of muff.

2. With larger crochet hook and 2 strands of **C** held tog, ch 7; then insert hook under (not through) 1st st at top right corner of muff, and sc 1.

3. Sc 1 under next st on edge, skip 3rd st, *sc 1 in each of next 2 sts, skip 3rd; rep from * to end of row—28 sc total.

4. Make absolutely sure that your last sc is in very last st on edge (if it's not, skip 1 or 2 sts to put it there); then ch 1, and FO.

5. Now turn piece 180° so that opposite long edge is on top. Rep steps 2–4, but start immediately with 1st sc and save those 7 ch until the end. In other words, insert your hook under 1st st of edge row, and sc 1. Sc to end of row, skipping each 3rd st— 28 sc total. Make sure that last sc is in very last st on edge, then ch 7, and FO. (This makes extra flaps for both cuffs to "button down" in same direction.)

Picking Up and Building On

1. With smaller needles, pick up all crocheted sts (see page 55 for instructions) along left side of muff (1st side you crocheted). Count to make sure you have 35 sts (28 sc + 7 ch) on needle.

2. Rib 5 rows, holding 2 strands of **B** tog: beg with k 1, p 1 on row 1; then k the knits and p the purls on rows 2–5.

3. BO in patt.

4. Rep on other side of muff, picking up all sc sts before you pick up ch sts. When you're done, use hook to hide all tails.

Stitch Together

You're not actually going to sew anything here. Instead, you'll single crochet the top and bottom edges of the muff together, right side out, using 2 strands of **C**, as you did in crocheting the cuffs on, so that you have a nice, purty crocheted seam (of sorts) running along the top of your muff. You *won't* close up the cuffs at this point, so don't do any single crocheting in the ribbing, OK? You'll get to those in a minute.

1. Fold muff in center, RS out, and line up CO and BO rows as neatly as possible. Use a few safety or straight pins to hold sides tog. (And some of you are going to fold muff WS out, so check again.)

2. Holding 2 strands of **C**, insert larger hook through 1st CO and BO sts at top edge of St st (not the ribbing!), pull through, and ch 1.

3. Sc 1 through each foll pair of CO and BO sts, being very careful to crochet through both.

4. Count to make sure you have 25 sc at end; then ch 1, and FO.

Sew on Buttons

Thread sewing needle with **C**. Wrap extra ribbed flap around cuff as you would a buttoned shirt cuff. Hold flap firmly tog with cuff rib, and sew button on through both flap and cuff (this will hold flap in place). Make sure not to sew through all 3 parts of rib—flap, and both sides of cuff—you'll sew your hand right out of the muff. One side is quite enough to nail that flap down. Rep for other cuff.

Block Garment

It's not necessary, but you can iron the intarsia just a little to flatten it out and straighten up the stitches. See page 25 for more guidelines.

Curious about why I went for the shirt-cuff look? There are several ways to create a cuff on a muff, and I chose this one for a practical reason, aside from the fact that I really like the buttons. Ribbing with circular needles seems like the most obvious way to do the cuff, but with such a small circle, it doesn't work well. You could knit the rib working with 4 needles at once, the way you would knit socks, but that's about as hard as it sounds. (You don't see any socks in this book, do you?) Put simply, this was the easiest way, and it doesn't look too shabby, either.

All-Organic Tote Bag

Well, actually it's not made from all-organic materials, but it has a very modern, natural look and is kind of dainty in a coarse, foresty way. Its real strength is a tight knit that makes the old-fashioned bag lining obsolete and produces a sturdy bag that will never lose even your dinkiest doohickey.

knit in the round	page 9
multistranding	page 51
raised stitches	page 44
crochet	page 3
picking up and building on	page 55
knit	page 9
fringes	page 58
sewing	page 24

SIZE

width: 12"

length: 8½–9"

MATERIALS

Schachenmayr nomotta Boston (70% acrylic, 30% wool; 1.75 oz, 60 yds), colors **A** #31 wehrot—1 ball, and **B** #58 petrol—3 balls

Schachenmayr nomotta Regia 6 Ply Color (75% wool, 25% polyamide; 1.75 oz, 137 yds), color C #5030 wit color—1 ball

1 button/knob of your choice

3' leather strip, very thin

5' soft rope, at least 1½" thick

8 mm straight knitting needles

5 mm, 32" circular needle

2–3 mm and 5 mm crochet hooks

sewing needle (size that fits your button)

safety/straight pins

GAUGE

stockinette stitch width: 2 sts=1", length: 3 rows=1"

rib width: 3 sts=1", length: 5 rows=1"

Overview

First you knit the front, top to bottom, in stockinette stitch, working in the raised pattern in the middle. Then you add a "natural fold" and work the back of the bag from the bottom up. You stitch the sides of the bag together on the outside, leaving a visible crocheted seam, and then crochet around the top, pick up those stitches, and build on the rib at the top with the circular needle. Finish it all off by sewing on the button, fastening on the tie, and knotting in the shoulder strap.

You'll use 3 knitting techniques to avoid the need for an old-fashioned lining (so frustrating to sew in). To make an extra tight, sturdy knit bag that won't pass your goodies through like a gallstone every time you wave or wiggle, use them all: (1) obviously, work your stitches very tightly, no matter what you're knitting with or how; (2) use thin needles for a tight knit; and (3) knit with several strands of yarn together so that each strand fills up holes that the other strands might leave. These 3 combined make a tote bag that's tighter than 5 o'clock traffic in L.A.

Directions

Front

Base Row Using straight needles and holding tog 1 strand each of **B** and **C**, CO 25 sts.

Rows 1–6 Work in St st, beg with a k row.

Rows 7–21 Raised Diamond Shape Pay attention to the logic behind this simple shape: basically, you've got 2 triangles, 1 pointing up and 1 pointing down. You're knitting from top to bottom, so you're starting at up-pointing triangle. That means you need to make 1 raised st on 1st row, 3 raised sts on 2nd row, 5 raised sts on 3rd row, and so on. (You increase by 2 on each row to add 1 to each side of triangle; if you added them 1 at a time, you'd have something like wacky Christmas tree lights. I don't recommend trying it.)

So, if your last row was a p row (it was), and if you cast on 25 sts (you did), do the math and check it with these directions to see if you can figure this out on your own next time.

Row 7: K 12, p 1, k 12.

Row 8: P 11, k 3, p 11.

Row 9: K 10, p 5, k 10.

Row 10: P 9, k 7, p 9.

Row 11: K 8, p 9, k 8.

Row 12: P 7, k 11, p 7.

Row 13: K 6, p 13, k 6.

Row 14: P 5, k 15, p 5.

Count 'em up, ladies (and gentlemen): 25 stitches on every row. You've reached the center, the widest part of the diamond, and now you start knitting the upside-down triangle. Before you do, though, remember that this is a diamond, not really 2 triangles. So, start working your way backwards from row 13, not row 14. That's because a diamond is 2 triangles that *share a base*. The base of your 1st triangle is row 14 (obviously); you don't need to knit it again.

Rows 15–21: Rep rows 13–7 in reverse order, and revel a little in the mathematical understanding you never thought you had.

Rows 22–28 Cont in St st for 7 rows, beg and ending with p rows.

Row 29 "Natural" Fold (What I am about to say is not a typo.) P all across.

What just happened? Be patient, knit a few more rows, and I'll show you. From this point on, you're knitting the entire pattern in reverse, but I'll write it out for you, just so you feel safe.

Row 29: "Natural Fold"

Back

Rows 30–36 Cont in St st for 7 rows, beg and ending with p rows.

Now have a look at the 3 purl rows that are side by side. Look at them from the outside of the bag (knit side with purl raised diamond) and notice that the 1st and 3rd purl rows blend in oh-so-nicely with the knit rows beside them (check the photo above to make sure yours really looks like that). Now look on the inside of the bag, and be amazed! The bumps that the 1st and 3rd purl rows make on the inside naturally fall into the space created by the purl row between them, whose bumps are on the outside. This creates a "natural" fold in the knitting, and you can make one anytime simply by knitting a purl row or purling a knit row in any stockinette stitch pattern.

(It works well for collars or cuffs that you want to roll back naturally, for instance.)

Rows 37–51 Knit diamond patt again: rep rows 7–21. (You can also just continue in St st for 15 rows if you want a diamond only on front of bag . . . or back, if you're the secretive type. Just be sure to beg and end with a k row.)

Rows 52–57 Cont in St st for 6 rows, beg with p row and ending with k row.

BO in p.

Stitch Together

You're going to crochet on the outside of the bag to make visible seams, so fold the bag right side out at the "natural" fold. Line up the sides of the bag, and place safety or straight pins along the edges—not *on* the edges, because you'll need to stitch there—to hold them in place. Line up the stitches as exactly as you can to get the straightest, most even seam possible (your reputation as a knitter depends on this—and we all know how important that is).

1. Insert larger crochet hook betw 1st and 2nd sts of 1st row from bottom and through same hole on other side; latch around **B**. Pull yarn through both holes, and ch 1. This fastens the yarn into place.

2. Insert hook betw 1st and 2nd sts of 2nd row on both sides, pull yarn through holes, and sc 1.

(Now's when you beg the real—pretty—seam.) Rep sc betw next pairs of sts all up side of bag until last (top) row; FO through this top hole.

3. Rep steps 1 and 2 on other edge of bag, then turn bag WS out, and hide tails.

Build On Rib

Short and sweet:

1. Holding just 1 strand of **A**, insert larger crochet hook under 1st CO st (or you could start at 1st BO st) at top of bag, ch 1, *insert hook under next st to left, and sc 1; rep all around bag's opening, skipping over sts you sewed through. At end, sl st 1 under ch at beg of rnd, and FO.

2. Pick up all crocheted sts on circular needle (see page 55 for how to do this).

3. Rib 7 rnds with **A** yarn, beg with k 1, p 1.

4. BO in rib using 5 mm crochet hook (instructions for this are on page 22), and hide tails with 2–3 mm hook.

Attach Button, Tie, and Strap

1. Place your button about 1/2" below ribbing on front of bag. Sew it on same as any old button.

2. Insert rope near side seams keeping toward back of bag. About 1 st beyond seam is good (see photo on page 132, "Inserting the Rope"). You

Inserting the Rope

Attaching the Leather Strap

can't insert it directly on seam, and inserting it on front of bag would make bag pooch inward, which is hardly attractive. Pull ends from inside of bag through to outside, and make a good, sturdy knot on the outside.

3. To fasten leather strap to back of bag, follow instructions for attaching fringes on page 58 (see photo above). You can make a (relatively) permanent bow in strap (so that you can just pull it around button every time). Or you can leave ends hanging, if you get your kicks off tying bows all day long.

Tyler Bucket Bag

This is a delicate little summer bag to tote around whenever you're wearing a girlish little floral dress. It's actually deceptively dainty; its true size will probably shock you. The mouth opens so wide it reminds me of Steven Tyler, but it's cute enough for Liv, so it just gets the family name.

Overview

First you have to punch holes in the leather round so that you can crochet onto it. Then you'll build up from a base row on those holes, working in a shell pattern for most of the bag and increasing the circumference as you go. At the end you'll sew on the straps and weave in the ties, and that's all there is to it.

Directions

Prepare Leather Round

You need to punch 69 holes in the leather round. The perimeter of your circle should be about 22", so, to evenly space the holes, you'll leave about ¹/₃" (about 8.5 mm) between them. Measure the round, and mark with a pen where you want to punch the holes. Punch them about ¹/₅" (about 5 mm) in from the edge. Use a 3 mm setting or head on the leather punch (that will be the size of the holes themselves).

If you can't get exactly 69 in evenly, don't sweat it. I'll tell you how to work with more or fewer holes in just a second.

Build Up Crochet

Foundation

1. Hold leather round with its rough, unfinished side (this will be WS) facing you. Hold **C** under it, and insert smaller hook from above through 1 hole

(see photo right). Yo and pull through hole to top of round to create 1 loop on hook.

2. *Insert hook through next hole to the left, draw yarn through hole, and sl st 1 (see photo right); rep from * all around, creating final sl st betw last hole and 1st hole to complete rnd—69 total sl sts (or however many holes you have).

3. Sl st 1 through 1st st at beg of rnd to fasten down yarn. Cut yarn, leaving approx 2" tail to be hidden away later; draw tail and other (beg) strand of yarn through to inside of leather round, and knot 2 tog.

Rnd 1

1. Using smaller hook and holding **C** under leather round, join yarn under 1st sl st (not through perforation!) of foundation, and ch 1 to build height.

2. *Insert hook through next st to left, and sc 1 (see photo on page 136, "Round 1"); rep from * to end of rnd. You want 69 sc sts on rnd 1, no matter how many holes you punched. If you couldn't fit 69 holes in the leather, just sc 2 through same sl st here and there (evenly scattered) to inc to 69. If you've got more than 69 holes, skip 1 sl st here and there (evenly) to dec to 69.

3. End with 1 sl st under ch at beg of rnd.

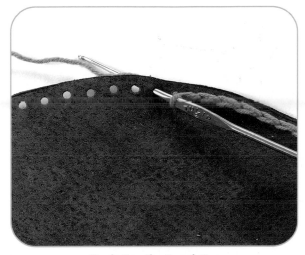

Crocheting the Foundation

Rnd 2: Shells

1. Using larger hook and **B**, join yarn in 1st st, and ch 3, dc 2, ch 2, dc 3—all under the same sc.

2. *Yo, insert hook into 3rd sc from hook, then dc 3, ch 2, dc 3. Rep from * to end of rnd—23 shells total.

3. End with 1 sl st in 3rd ch at beg of this rnd.

Rnds 3–7: Shells

1. Sl st 1 through each of 1st 3 sts of 1st shell to reach top of that shell, then FO **B** yarn.

2. With larger hook, join **A**, and ch 3, dc 2, ch 2, dc 3 (all under 2 ch sts that join dc groups in center of 1st shell).

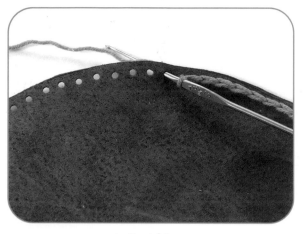

Round 1

3. *Insert hook through center of next shell (hole under 2 ch sts that join dc groups), then dc 3, ch 2, dc 3; rep * to end of rnd—23 shells total.

4. End with 1 sl st in 3rd ch at beg of rnd. Rep for next 4 rnds, and then FO.

Rnds 8–10: Shells Join B, and rep rnds 3–7.

For round 11, which will top off your bag with a nice frilly edging, you can insert your hook either into the hole between the 2 sides of a shell, or into the chain stitches themselves. On the outer sides of a shell, you should insert the hook in (not under) the double-crochet stitches themselves.

Rnd 11: Fans

1. Using smaller hook and **C**, insert hook into 1st st

of prev rnd, *ch 3, hdc 1; insert hook into next st, sc 1, ch 2, hdc 1; insert hook into next st and rep from * to end of rnd.

2. End with 1 sl st in 1st hdc at beg of rnd, and FO.

Attach Straps and Weave In Ties

You can, of course, attach the straps anywhere you want, but you'll probably find the traditional placement the most practical: with either end of a single strap on opposite sides of the bag and the other strap right next to it (leaving a couple of stitches between them). If you do it this way (and that's how I did it), make sure it's symmetrical by counting that you have the same number of stitches (or shells) between the 2 ends of each strap and the same 2 or so shells between the straps at each side.

Also count to insert the ties right in the middle of the big space between 2 ends of a single strap, since that will become the front of your bag.

1. Set leather punch to make 3 mm holes, and punch 8 holes in each end of wider leather strips, creating 2 squares with holes as corners (see photo on page 137, "Attaching the Straps").

2. Holding 1 strap end over top pink row of bag where you want to fasten it, use sewing needle with **C** to attach it to bag, using crisscross sts through bottom 4 holes of the strap and through crochet work of bag. Make several sts through

Attaching the Straps

Weaving In the Ties

holes to be sure strap won't fall off (see photo above). Knot yarn on inside of bag, and hide ends. Rep to attach rem 3 strap ends.

3. With **C**, sew cross sts through rem 4 holes at ends of each strap, fastening straps sturdily to top crochet row of bag. Knot yarn on inside of bag, and sew away ends.

4. Holding 2 thinner leather strips tog, use larger crochet hook to weave them into next-to-last row of shells at top of bag (see photo above).

5. Turn bag WS out, and use smaller hook to hide rem yarn ends.

Pippi's Fishnet Skirt

On one of Pippi Longstocking's many adventures at sea, I distinctly remember her dressed almost entirely in fishing nets. To make this skirt, I had to clean that look up a little, but luckily the crocheted net pattern gives an authentic feeling of strong, thick rope when it's made holding 2 strands of yarn together. It takes on a double-helix-like twisty effect that's not only pretty darn close to Pippi's original dress but also strong enough to hold up to just her types of adventures.

crochet .... page 3

parallel net .... page 36

multistranding .... page 51

turning corners .... page 33

SIZE

S (M, L, XL)

waist circumference: 28" (30", 32", 34")

circumference at bottom: 52" (56", 60", 64")

length: 27–28"

The skirt is elastic and will stretch at the waist, but it should hug your midriff pretty snugly.

MATERIALS

Schachenmayr nomotta Aurora (55% cotton, 45% acrylic; 1.75 oz, 98 yds) colors **A** #73 pistazie—5 (S, M) or 6 (L, XL) balls, **B** #21 lemon—1 ball, and **C** #22 sonne—1 ball

Gedifra Florida (50% cotton, 50% acrylic; 1.75 oz, 142 yds), color **D** #1407—1 ball

1 big button, approx 1½" in diameter

1 small button, approx 1" in diameter

2–3 mm and 5 mm crochet hooks

sewing needle (size that fits your buttons)

You need to split 1 ball each of **B** and **C** into 2 balls. (Don't unravel the whole ball of yarn: just start rolling a new ball, and, when you see that it's about the same size as the ball that's left, cut the yarn. They don't have to be exact.) Or just buy an extra ball of each, which I recommend, because you always need extra yarn anyway.

Size S and M knitters also need to split their 5th ball of **A** into 2 balls.

GAUGE

waistband width: 3 sc or ch=1", length: 5 sc rows=2"

net length: 1 dc=1"

If you want the skirt longer, just follow the pattern for the last row (without increasing) to keep adding rows until you're happy.

Overview

All right. This is intense. You crochet a classic net pattern for the body of the skirt, from the top down, increasing the width and length of the garment by increasing the sides (height) and bases (width) of the rectangles on each row. Then you add a waistband, crochet a pretty intricate flower, and attach that by a method you're never going to forget (and never going to want to do again). You add the button, give a sigh of relief, and exclaim that it was totally worth it.

Remember that it's a net pattern, which means it's full of holes. Don't even think about joining yarn in the middle of a row. Check at the beginning of each row that you've got enough to finish! (See page 8 for more on joining yarn.)

Directions

Base Row Holding 2 strands of **A** tog, ch 85 (90, 95, 100) with larger hook.

Row 1 Flip your work, and ch 1 to build height, then sc 1 through each st of prev row—85 (90, 95, 100) sc total.

Row 2

1. Flip your work, and ch 4 for height, then ch 6 more for width.

2. Tr 1 in 5th st from hook.

3. *Ch 6, then tr 1 in 5th st from hook. Rep from * 15x (16x, 17x, 18x)—16 (17, 18, 19) tr total.

Row 3

1. Flip your work, and ch 4 for height, then ch 6 more for width.

2. Tr 1 in last tr of prev row.

3. *Ch 6, then tr 1 in next tr of prev row. Rep from * 15x (16x, 17x, 18x)—16 (17, 18, 19) tr total.

What you've made so far are just 2 rows in the pattern, with space between them for your hips to slip into this skirt. You'll put a button on there later, but now you're going to connect the beginning and end of this row so you can crochet the rest of the skirt working in a circle. (Don't get confused by the fact that I start calling them rounds, either.)

4. Insert hook into corner st (4th ch from beg of row 3), and sl st 1.

OK. From now on, you'll work just on 1 side of the skirt, without flipping your work. Let's get to it.

Rnds 4–5

1. Ch 6 for height and 7 for width.

2. Dtr 1 in 1st tr of prev rnd.

3. *Ch 7, then dtr 1 through next tr of prev rnd. Rep from * 14x (15x, 16x, 17x)—15 (16, 17, 18) dtr total.

4. Ch 7, insert your hook in corner of 1st rectangle of this rnd (6th ch from beg), and sl st 1 to connect rnd.

Rnds 6–7

1. Ch 6 for height and 8 for width.

2. Dtr 1 in 1st dtr of prev rnd.

3. *Ch 8, then dtr 1 through next dtr of prev rnd. Rep from * 14x (15x, 16x, 17x)—15 (16, 17, 18) dtr total.

4. Ch 8, insert hook in corner of 1st rectangle of this rnd (6th ch from beg), and sl st 1 to connect rnd.

Rnds 8–9

1. Ch 8 for height and 9 for width.

2. Trtr 1 in 1st dtr of prev rnd.

3. *Ch 9, then trtr 1 through next dtr of prev rnd. Rep from * 14x (15x, 16x, 17x).

4. Ch 9, insert hook in corner of 1st rectangle of rnd (8th ch from beg), and sl st 1 to connect rnd.

Rnds 10–11

1. Ch 8 for height and 10 for width.

2. Trtr 1 in 1st trtr of prev rnd.

3. *Ch 10, then trtr 1 through next trtr of prev rnd. Rep from * 14x (15x, 16x, 17x).

4. Ch 10, insert hook in corner of 1st rectangle of rnd (8th ch from beg), and sl st 1 to connect rnd.

Rnds 12–14

1. Ch 10 for height and 11 for width.

Now you're going to do something for which traditional crocheting has no technical term. I call it "double treble treble crochet"... but that probably doesn't tell you much. (It's not entirely accurate, either.) Basically, when you treble treble crochet, you yarn over and slip through 4 times, right? Do these 5 times here. I'm going to abbreviate this "quintr" and hope that you remember that "quint" is the Latin root for 5. Ready?

2. Quintr 1 in trtr (quintr on rows 13–14) of prev rnd.

3. *Ch 11, then quintr 1 through next trtr (quintr on rows 13–14) of prev rnd. Rep from * 14x (15x, 16x, 17x).

4. Ch 11, insert hook in corner of 1st rectangle of rnd (10th ch from beg), and sl st 1 to connect rnd.

Rnd 15

1. Ch 10 for height and 12 for width.

2. Quintr 1 in 1st quintr of prev rnd.

3. *Ch 12, then quintr 1 through next quintr of prev rnd. Rep from * 14x (15x, 16x, 17x).

4. Ch 12, insert your hook in corner of 1st rectangle of rnd (10th ch from beg), and sl st 1 to connect rnd.

FO

Crochet Waistband

The inside and outside of your skirt are different, so look closely, choose the side you like better, and from now on work with it right side out. You should lay the skirt flat, with the gap at the waist on your left. The photo on page 142, "Crocheting the Gap," is your guide for working your way around the gap.

1. Holding tog strands from 2 balls you made of **B**, insert larger hook from above into st at top back corner of gap at waist; pull yarn through, and ch 1.

2. Insert hook into 1st ch on base row of skirt, pull yarn through, and sc 1.

Crocheting the Gap

9. Sc 3 through hole in upper rectangle.

10. Sc 1 through 1st ch on 1st row of skirt.

11. Sc 1 in corner st (last ch of base row).

Unless you're a real masochist, I expect you moved the garment around as you worked to make the stitching easier, so the gap should now be on your right.

12. Sc 1 in each of base row ch sts along waist of skirt—85 (90, 95, 100) sc total (not counting gap sc sts).

You should be back at the corner of the gap where you started.

13. Sl st 1 under 1st ch you made in waist and gap row.

14. Ch 8 (to make button loop), then insert hook under 1st ch in waist again, sl st 1, and FO. (If diameter of your button is smaller—or larger—than the recommended 1", ch fewer or more than 8 sts to adjust size of button loop.)

Crochet Flower

Center

1. Hold 2 balls you made of **B** tog, and, using larger hook, ch 8. Sl st 1 through 1st ch to connect sts into a circle.

3. To work edge of gap, insert hook into hole—not ch sts that make up its side—of 1st rectangle forming side of gap, and sc 3.

4. Insert hook in little hole at end of 1st rectangle—where 2 rectangles join and create a little circle—and sc 1.

5. Insert hook in hole—not ch sts—of next rectangle (below), and sc 3.

6. Insert hook in base st of gap (where you joined rows into a circle), and sc 1.

7. Sc 3 in hole of lower rectangle on 2nd side of gap.

8. Sc 1 in hole where lower and upper rectangles join.

2. Ch 1 for height, then sc 12 through center of circle—not through ch sts themselves. Sl st 1 through 1st sc to join rnd.

Petals

3. Ch 8, then sl st 1 through 2nd sc from hook. This is 1st petal. (Your petals won't all be the same size.)

4. Ch 9, and sl st 1 through 2nd sc from hook.

5. Ch 10, and sl st 1 through 2nd sc from hook. Rep 1x to make 2 petals this size.

6. Ch 9, and sl st 1 through 2nd sc from hook.

7. Ch 8, and sl st 1 through 2nd sc from hook.

Now you'll work from inside each petal to buff up their borders.

8. In each petal, make as many sc sts as you have ch sts for that petal (for example, 8 for 1st petal, 9 for next, 10 for next 2). Make your sc sts through center of petal, not through ch sts themselves. At end of each petal, sl st 1 through same sc you sl st through when making petal itself (in steps 3–7 above).

9. FO, and pull yarn through to back of flower (the side you made the sl sts on is front).

Stem

10. In 1 hand, hold both flower (RS up) and 2 strands of **C** tog. Insert your larger hook from above into 1 of holes betw 2 petals and center of flower, pull yarn through hole, sl st 1 to fasten it into place, and then ch 120. FO.

Don't worry. I didn't forget anything. You're going to add that chic yellow streak through the golden stem as you attach the flower.

As you fasten the flower to the skirt, pay close attention, because there are a few things you need to pay close attention to:

* Don't single crochet through both the flower and the skirt in any spot where the flower doesn't naturally fall on top of a junction of rectangles on the skirt. You don't want to reach with the hook or stretch the yarn, because this will force your skirt out of shape. Then the skirt won't fall as nicely (it won't fall nicely at all, in fact), and some part is likely to tear with time.

* Generally attach each petal in only 1 spot (preferably near the rounded top), although you can do it twice if a suitable spot happens naturally.

* In each spot where you attach the petals, single crochet only once through both the flower and the skirt; make the 2nd single crochet only through the petal.

* When attaching any part of the flower to the skirt, make sure you insert your hook through one of the stitches in the skirt—not just through one of

the "ropes" that make up a side of a rectangle—otherwise the stitch will shift around as you move.

✳ Attach the leaves to the skirt rather strategically so that they don't flop around and fall out of shape. Pay attention to where you can make a leaf without warping the shape of your skirt: find places where there are stitches in the skirt at both the base and the tip of the leaf.

Attach Flower and Buttons

Congratulations! You have reached the most challenging technique in this book. Don't fret, though, you'll get through it with me (and maybe with a little help from your more experienced crocheting friends). To start, just lay the skirt on a flat surface, with right side out and front side facing up.

1. Place flower where you want to attach it, and place big button in center of flower. (Center of button has to fall on a junction of 4 rectangles, so that you can sew it closely around cross formed there.) Holding skirt, flower, and button tog firmly, so they don't shift out of place, turn skirt WS out, and sew button onto skirt with sewing needle and **D**. Fasten center of flower onto skirt with sewing needle as well.

2. Holding (just 1 strand of) **D** under petals of flower, insert your smaller hook into 1 of sc sts betw 2 petals, pull yarn through, and ch 1.

3. Working around petal, sc 2 in each yellow sc st of edge of petal to give it a dark yellow border. When you reach end of 1 petal, sc 1 through st there, then cont to sc 2 through each yellow sc around next petal. (There's not enough room for 2 sc betw petals.) Read step 4 before you beg this step.

4. As you work around entire flower this way, where possible insert hook both through sc in flower and through a st in skirt (see photo on page 145, "Attaching Flower Petals to Skirt"), pull yarn through both sts, and sc as usual.

5. Once you've made it all around flower, sl st 1 through 1st st you made (in step 2), and FO.

6. Insert hook from above at top of the stem (where you joined it to flower), but not through skirt. Still working with 1 strand of **D**, sl st 1 through each ch of stem. Where possible, sl st through both stem and a st in skirt, to fasten stem down (see photo on page 145, "Attaching Stem and Leaves to Skirt"). You don't need to do this often, but you do need to follow the 5 points I give in the sidebar (pages 143–44) about not deforming the shape of your skirt. (Read them again if you have to. They're important.)

7. To make leaves, attach base of leaf (that would be where it starts to jut out from straight stem) to skirt, count 9 sl sts (through 9 ch sts in stem), attach tip of leaf to skirt as well (see "Attaching

Attaching Flower Petals to Skirt

Attaching Stem and Leaves to Skirt

Stem and Leaves to Skirt" above), count 9 more sl sts, then attach other side of leaf base to 1st side. You don't have to fasten 2nd part of leaf base to skirt, because it's attached to 1st, which is already attached to skirt. Just make sure to get both top and bottom parts of leaf base into this 1 sl st.

8. Make sure that last st of stem is fastened to skirt, then ch 1 and FO.

Sew smaller button onto corner of gap at waist, opposite loop you made earlier.

Block Garment

Your waistband needs to be straightened so that it won't twist all around your waist when you wear the skirt. Follow the instructions on page 25 for ironing knits if you don't know how.

When you're finished ironing, take a deep breath, slide this baby on, and do a little square dance—you're done!

Cinderella Skirt

I never saw the Disney movie, but in the original Grimm's fairy tale, Cinderella lived out in the country. That's probably why I always imagined her wearing a simple, comfortable, foresty-looking skirt like this. I'm not sure I would mop a floor in it, but it's definitely appropriate for going out to meet your godmother.

SIZE

S-M (L-XL)

body circumference at bottom: 58", length: 27 1/2"

waistband circumference: 28" (35"), length: 3"

Because you size the skirt only at the waistband, it hangs differently on different size people: on a small person, it's loose at the hips; on a large person, it's tighter (but slimming).

MATERIALS

Schachenmayr nomotta Two in One (32% wool, 5% nylon, 63% acrylic; 1.75 oz, 87 yds), color **A** #90 bouclé marmor—5 balls

Gedifra Tecno Hair Lungo (100% polyamide; 1.75 oz, 87 yds), 1 ball of each of colors **B** #9704, **C** #9712, and **D** #9703

Gedifra Fashion Trend (51% wool, 49% acrylic; 1.75 oz, 98 yds), color **E** #4904—2 balls

1 leather strip, 3 1/4' long

5 mm and 8 mm, 32" circular knitting needles

stitch marker/extra yarn (whatever you use to remind you where rounds begin)

2–3 mm and 3–4 mm crochet hooks

Winter skirts aren't exactly renowned for being flattering, so if you want to make this one look even more slimming, use a darker Schachenmayr Two in One yarn.

GAUGE

rib width: 5 sts=2", length: 4 rows=1"

stockinette stitch width: 4 sts=2", length: 4 rows=1"

Overview

You knit in the round from the bottom up, and make a few rows of extended stitches at the bottom. At the end you build on the waistband (which is where you size the skirt), make a little crocheted edging, and attach the waist tie.

This skirt has lots of holes, so see the section "Joining New Yarn" on page 15 before you start. It's a good candidate for the "drop, twist, and add" method of joining yarn, but the extended-stitch rows are pretty tall, so be sure to leave the yarn loose enough at the joining point if you choose to use it. Otherwise you'll scrunch up the extended stitches.

Directions

Base Rnd With larger needles and **A**, CO 150 sts. Check that they aren't twisted on the needle, and then connect them into a circle. (If you don't know how to do this, see page 43.) Add marker at beg of rnd.

Rnds 1–2 K all sts.

Rnd 3: Extended Stitches

1. Join **B**, and k 1.
2. *Yo twice, then k the next st as usual. (Don't skip any sts or do anything with yo wraps. Leave them betw k sts.) Rep from * to end of rnd.

Rnd 4: Extended Stitches

1. Join **A**, and k 1.
2. *Now unwrap double yo that you made on prev rnd; k next st as usual. Rep from * to end of rnd. (Be careful not to k your yo wraps or to lose your real sts as you unwrap.)

Rnds 5–6 K all sts (with **A**).

Rnds 7–8 Rep rnds 3–4, joining **C** for rnd 7 and switching back to **A** for rnd 8.

Rnds 9–10 K all sts (with **A**).

Rnds 11–12 Rep rnds 3–4, joining **D** for rnd 11 and switching back to **A** for rnd 12.

Rnds 13–14 K all sts (with **A**).

Rnd 15 K all sts (with **A**), dec 1 every 15th st. In other words, count 13 sts from beg of rnd, k sts 14 and 15 tog; *count next 13, k 2 tog; rep from * to end of rnd. At end, check that you have 140 sts.

Rnds 16–24 K all sts (with **A**).

Rnds 25–26 Rep rnds 3 and 4, joining **C** for rnd 25 and switching back to **A** for rnd 26.

Rnd 27 K all sts (with **A**), dec 1 every 14th st. In other words, count 12 sts from beg of rnd, k sts 13 and 14 tog; *count next 12, k 2 tog; rep from * to end of rnd. You should have 130 sts.

Rnds 28–47 K all sts (with **A**).

Rnd 48 K all sts (with **A**), dec 1 every 13th st: *count 11, k 2 tog; rep from * to end. You should have 120 sts.

Rnds 49–67 K all sts (with **A**).

Rnd 68 K all sts (with **A**), dec 1 every 12th st: *count 10, k 2 tog; rep from * to end. You should have 110 sts.

Rnds 69–87 K all sts (with **A**).

Rnd 88 K all sts (with **A**), dec 1 every 10th st: *count 8, k 2 tog; rep from * to end. You should have 100 sts.

Rnd 89 K all sts (with **A**).

BO (Whew!)

Now you're going to touch up the skirt with crocheting. Before you do, though, take a close look at both sides of your skirt and choose which side you want to be the right side. They're (very) different: because you knitted in the round, 1 side is all knit stitches and the other all purl stitches. It's slightly easier to crochet on the purl side, but those horizontal-running purls might create the illusion that you're a little wider than you really are, so try on the skirt each way, and see which you prefer. Once you choose the right side, work with it facing out (as you would wear it) from now on. Don't worry if the tails are on that side. You'll hide them later, and no one will be the wiser.

Build On Waistband

Try the skirt on real quick. If you can just barely get into it now, don't decrease any stitches in waistband. Just single crochet through every stitch without skipping any. (You'd be somewhere between XL and XXL, in this case.)

Decrease Waist

1. Holding **E** inside skirt, insert larger hook below 1st BO st at beg of rnd, pull yarn through, and ch 1.

2. Sc 1 under (not through) each BO st, dec 1 (that is, skipping) every 5th (10th) st—80 (90) sc total.

3. At end of rnd, sl st 1 under 1st ch you made, and FO.

Picking Up and Building On

1. Starting at beg of rnd, pick up all sc sts (through the back) with 5 mm circular needle.

You're going to build a simple ribbed waistband now, but you need to leave room for a gap so that you'll be able to slide this baby on. To do this, you're going to knit on the circular needle, but not in the round. How do you do this? Don't connect the rounds as you knit. That means you'll be knitting a flat piece in rows, and you'll flip your work at the end of each row.

2. **Row 1** Join **E** in 1st sc, and k 1, p 1 to end.

3. **Rows 2–12** Flip your work, then k the knits and p the purls. BO in rib.

Crochet Edging

For all the edging you'll need **E** and the larger hook.

Bottom: Shells

1. Insert hook under—not through— 1st CO st, and ch 4, tr 1, ch 2, and tr 2—all under same CO st.

2. *Tr 2 under 3rd st from your hook, then ch 2 and tr 2 under same st. Rep from * all around bottom of skirt, 49x—50 shells total.

3. Sl st 1 in 4th ch of 1st shell, and FO.

Waist: Fans

Make sure the skirt is laid out with the gap on your right. You're going to crochet around the top of the waistline first, then dip down into the gap. (This is important to remember so that you begin at the correct corner.)

1. Insert hook under BO st at corner of gap, then ch 3 and hdc 1 under same st.

2. *Skip 1 st in BO row of rib, then sc 1, ch 2, and hdc 1—all under same st. Rep from * until you reach other corner of skirt—39x (44x) total.

3. Crochet just as in step 2 all along edge of gap. Notice that gap is 12 sts (technically those are rows) high, so you'll do 6 fans on each side, first working down, then working back up. At end, FO.

Weave In Waist Tie

The leather strap ties closed the gap at the waist. To attach it, simply use the crochet hook to weave it through the crocheting along the gap (not the waist), beginning at 1 corner and ending at the other. (It's easiest to pull it through the hole that's just below the 2 chain stitches in each fan pattern. Spread the crocheting out a little, and look closely so you can see where I mean.

Going out to meet your fairy godmother in the sweltering summer heat? No problem. Just make the following substitutions:

* Instead of Schachenmayr Two in One, use Schachenmayr Aurora

* Instead of Gedifra Tecno Hair Lungo, use Gedifra Poesie

* Instead of Gedifra Fashion Trend, use Gedifra Florida

The skirt that you make with those should keep you nice and cool while all your dreams are coming true.

Skater Pants

Aaaah, the Skater Pants . . . crown of all things urban. Like the Beach Bandana on page 62, these are from my days as a stitch-everything-in-sight knitter. Comfortable as they are, knit pants could make Twiggy's butt look big, so I've made sure the hips in this design are knit in a dark color for a more slimming look.

✳ **ELEMENTS OF THIS DESIGN**

knit	page 9
multistranding	page 51
sewing	page 24
crochet	page 3
windows	page 37
picking up and building on	page 55
knit in the round	page 43
buttonholes	page 55
weaving in	page 59

SIZE

S (M-L)

total length: 27 1/2"

waistband circumference: 29" (33"),
length: 2 1/2"

crotch to bottom of waistband length: 10"

hips circumference: 36"

foot opening circumference: 22"

MATERIALS

Schachenmayr nomotta Aurora (55% cotton,
45% acrylic; 1.75 oz, 98 yds), colors **A** #03
sand—10 balls, and **B** #50 marine—6 balls

2 small buttons of your choice, maximum
2/5" (about 10 mm) in diameter

5 leather strips, two 3' long (optional),
three 10" long

8 mm straight knitting needles

5 mm, 32" circular knitting needle

2–3 mm and 5 mm crochet hooks

sewing needle (size that fits your buttons)

straight or safety pins

GAUGE

stockinette stitch width: 6 sts=2",
length: 4 rows=1"

rib width: 7 sts=2", length: 5 rows=1"

Overview

You knit the pants in 2 pieces, from bottom to top. The 1st piece will become the left leg and left side of the torso; the 2nd will be the right. When you're done, you immediately stitch them together; then you add a little crocheted edging around the foot holes, build on the waistband, and attach the belt loops and the optional leg ties.

You'll size the pants only in the waistband (just as you did for the Cinderella Skirt), so the body of them will be looser on a small than on a medium or large person.

As you knit the stripes, don't cut the yarn and join anew every time; just pull it along (see page 51), but be sure not to pull too tightly when you pick it up again, otherwise it will scrunch up your pants leg. When you're about to get into a big stretch of 1 yarn (where it's impossible—or at least very unwise—to carry the other yarn along), I'll tell you to cut and tie it. When you do cut, leave the tails as long as they can be without irritating you; they'll make stitching the 2 sides together much easier later on.

Knit the *whole* piece holding 2 strands of yarn together, for both colors. Only the crocheting ("sewing") will be done with just 1 strand.

Directions

Left Leg

Base Row Holding 2 strands of A tog, CO 70 sts onto straight needles.

Rows 1–2 Drop A, join 2 strands of B, and work in St st, beg with a p row.

Rows 3–4 Pick up A, and cont in St st.

Rows 5–6 Pick up B, and cont in St st.

Rows 7–11 Cut B, pick up A, and cont in St st for 5 rows.

Row 12 Cut A, pick up B, and cont in St st to end of row. Cut B. (You have to cut A at the beginning of this row because you knit only 1 row of B, leaving you at 1 end while A is still hanging at the other.)

Rows 13–65 Join 2 strands of A and cont in St st for 53 rows.

Rows 66–67 Drop A, join 2 strands of B, and cont in St st.

Rows 68–69 Pick up A, and cont in St st, then cut A, and FO.

Now you begin decreasing for your waist and shaping the curve under your bum. In order to decrease from both sides, you'll decrease at the beginning of every row. You'll use a simple, knit-2-together decrease that's just like binding off. (See page 52, if you think you've never done this. I'm willing to bet you have.)

Pay attention to the following facts about your work, because they have major consequences for how many decreases you'll make on each row: the purl side is the right side of the pants and this is the left leg, which means that the beginning of each purl row will wind up on your backside, while the beginning of each knit row will wind up on your front side. No matter who you are, your backside is bigger than your front, so you need to make a bigger curve there (translation: decrease more) than you do on the front. Notice that all your purl rows decrease a little more.

Rows 70–101 Pick up B, and cont in St st for 32 rows, dec on rows 71–79 as follows:

> Row 71: P sts 1 and 2 tog, p sts 2 and 3 tog, p sts 3 and 4 tog, p rem sts normally to end of row.

Row 72: K sts 1 and 2 tog, k sts 2 and 3 tog, k rem sts normally to end of row.

Row 73: Rep row 71.

Row 74: Rep row 72.

Row 75: P sts 1 and 2 tog, p sts 2 and 3 tog, p rem sts normally to end of row.

Row 76: K sts 1 and 2 tog, k rem sts normally to end of row.

Row 77: Rep row 75.

Row 78: Rep row 76.

Row 79: P sts 1 and 2 tog, p rem sts normally to end of row.

Rows 102–106 Cut **B**, join **A**, and cont in St st for 5 rows.

BO in p.

Right Leg

Now that you've finished the left leg, all you need to do to make the right leg is knit it *exactly* the same as the left one, with the exception of rows 71–80, in which you decrease as follows:

Row 71 P sts 1 and 2 tog, p sts 2 and 3 tog, p rem sts normally to end of row.

Row 72 K sts 1 and 2 tog, k sts 2 and 3 tog, k sts 3 and 4 tog, k rem sts normally to end of row.

Row 73 Rep row 71.

Row 74 Rep row 72.

Row 75 P sts 1 and 2 tog, p rem sts normally to end of row.

Row 76 K sts 1 and 2 tog, k sts 2 and 3 tog, k rem sts normally to end of row.

Row 77 Rep row 75.

Row 78 Rep row 76.

Row 79 P all sts to end of row.

Row 80 K sts 1 and 2 tog, k rem sts normally to end of row.

Why the switch? This is the right leg, which puts the beginning of the knit stitches on your butt this time.

Stitch Together

You'll use the smaller crochet hook to slip stitch the 2 legs together and to close them up. Use the long tails you left on the garment (just 1 strand at a time), beige for beige portions and blue for blue portions. If you have to, you can use the other color on a short stripe (such as beige yarn to sew up just 2 rows of blue), but don't do it on longer stretches or the sewing is likely to show through.

As you stitch, be especially careful to get your hook into the 2nd stitch on each row, not the 1st, because sewing along the edge stitches would leave holes in your seams, which you don't want running

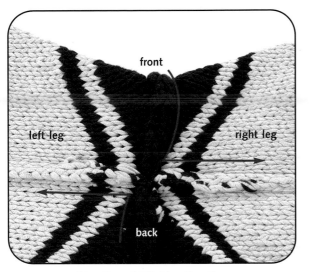

Direction of Stitching Together

2. Insert hook into 2nd pair of sts on next row below, and sl st 1.

3. Sl st 1 in each foll pair of sts until you reach next-to-last blue row on hips (where you began to dec). Sl st 1 in next-to-last blue row as well, but not in last blue row.

Right Leg

4. Pull edges of right leg tog, k side out, and cont to sl st down right leg. When you reach CO row, sl st 1 through 2nd pair of sts as usual, then ch 1 and FO.

Turn the pants so that the backside is now to your left.

Back

1. Rep steps 1–3 of front stitching up. In last blue row at hips, sl st 1 through the same st (2nd st on row) in *all 4 pieces* of pants, to join them tog

Left Leg

2. Rep step 4 of right leg.

Crochet Edging: Windows

Now turn the pants right side (purl side) out, and lay them upside down so that you can work comfortably along the leg openings at the bottom.

1. Holding 2 strands of **B** tog, insert your larger hook under 1st st on inside corner (where you stitched tog on CO row) of 1 leg, pull yarn through, ch 2, then hdc 1 in 2nd st from hook.

along your pants legs (and definitely not in the crotch). Have a look at the edge stitches where you decreased, and you'll see why.

Lay the 2 pieces 1 on top of the other, with purl sides together and knit sides facing out. The butt of the pants is the side with more curve (because you decreased more there); place it to your right. Before you begin stitching up, take a close look at the photo above and don't hesitate to refer back to it as much as necessary as you go.

Front

1. At top left corner of pants, insert crochet hook into 2nd st on 1st row (BO row), and through same stitch in other leg; pull yarn through sts.

2. *Ch 1 and hdc 1 in 2nd st from hook; rep from * to end of rnd—34x total.

3. At end of rnd, ch 1, insert hook in 2nd ch st at beg, and sl st 1; FO.

4. Rep for other leg. Hide tails with your smaller hook.

Build On Waistband

With the pants still right side out, lay them front side up with the waist on top. You're going to add a ribbed lining to the waist, with a button-close flap on the left side of the pants (the side lying to your right at the moment). Straighten out the pants as much as possible, because you'll knit the gap in your waistband where the crease between front and back at the right side is now. Try to get the crease to fall right in the middle of the side of the leg.

1. Holding 2 strands of **B** tog, insert larger hook under the BO st that falls at crease in top right corner of waist, pull yarn through, and ch 1.

2. Insert hook under next st to left, and sc 1. Now here's the only difference in the entire patt betw S and M (L):

   S Cont sc 1 under each BO st to end of row, skipping each 17th st and sts that you sewed through in front and back—95 sc total + 1 ch.

M (L) Cont sc 1 below each BO st to end of row, skipping over sts that you sewed through in front and back—101 sc total + 1 ch.

3. At end of rnd, ch 12, and FO.

4. Pick up all sts—1st ch, 95 (101) sc, and last 12 ch—on circular needle. (See page 55 if you don't know how to pick up stitches.)

5. Rib 10 rows (with 2 strands of **B**), dec for buttonholes as foll:

   Row 1: P 1, k 1 to end.

   Row 2: K the knits and p the purls.

   Row 3: P 1, k 1, p 1, then skp (that is, slip 4th st off onto right needle without knitting it, p 5th st as usual, use left needle to pass 4th st over 5th st and drop it off needle—just as you do when you BO); cont in rib (beg with k) to end of row.

   Row 4: Rib 93 (99) sts, then CO 1 (just as you do at beg of a piece, with the fingerwork and all); cont in rib (beg with p) to end of row.

   Rows 5–6: K the knits and p the purls.

   Rows 7–8: Rep rows 3–4, respectively.

   Rows 9–10: K the knits and p the purls.

6. BO in rib, and use smaller crochet hook to hide all tails.

Placement of Buttons and Belt Loops

stitches so that the ends wind up on the outside of the pants. Now bring your hand outside as well and tie the knot on the outside.

Where to insert them? They look best around the beige stripe at the top of the knitting, with 1 end popping out from between the blue and beige stitches at the top of the stripe and the other from between the blue and beige yarns at the bottom of the stripe (see photo, "Placement of buttons and belt loops"). You want to put 1 on the back seam and 1 on each hip, but fold the pants neatly before you do the sides, so that you find the perfect center along each side crease. Once you've got the strips in the holes, don't just knot the 2 ends together: hold the 2 ends together, and then tie a knot with them both.

Sew On Buttons

Sew your buttons onto the ribbed waist, at about the 8th stitch in from the gap (see photo above). You can put the pants on to find just the right spot for the buttons, but be careful not to stretch the knitting as you pull the flap closed. (If you do, you're likely to rip open the buttonholes the first time you actually button your pants closed.) Place a safety or straight pin in the holes to mark the button positions until you can sew the buttons on.

Attach Belt Loops

The belt loops are the short leather strips. To attach them, hold them inside the pants (while the pants are right side out), and insert them through the

Weave In Leg Ties (Optional)

If you want to be able to tie closed the leg openings, weave 1 of the long leather strips into each leg opening, using a hook to work it through the holes in the crocheted edging. Be sure to start on the outer side of each leg so that you'll be able to tie it and the bows (or the knots, if you're hardcore) will show. (Never woven in ties before? See page 59.)

Block Garment

Ironing the seams along the legs will straighten them out considerably. See page 25 for instructions on how to do it without burning a hole in the crotch.

Her Clogs

Rubber clogs are the most popular kitchen shoes for modern chefs. They keep every-thing that spills and spatters off the feet and are easily wiped or hosed down after work. I saw a lot of people wearing them in the streets, and they always caught my eye: they seemed just like simple work shoes, but they came in the most outrageous colors, and that made me think they had design potential. I bought a pair, punched some holes in them, and started to see what I could do.

They're now my hottest seller, and hard as I try I can't keep up with the demand. You can do absolutely anything with them: I punch decorative holes, attach crocheted flowers, animal faces, socks, and even interchangeable appliqués. I'm giving you a simple flower pattern, just so you can get a feel for working with the clogs. Once you've got it down, pick your favorite object in the world, stitch it up, and stick it on there. You can wear your obsessions everywhere and expand your shoe collection expo-nentially all at the same time.

ELEMENTS OF THIS DESIGN

crochet	page 3
picking up and building on	page 55

SIZE

The size of the shoes depends on your feet. The size of the flower really doesn't matter.

MATERIALS

Gedifra Florida (50% cotton, 50% acrylic; 1.75 oz, 142 yds), choose any 2 or 3 colors, **A** and **B** (and **C**), that go with the color of your clogs (I used #1420 and #1445)—1 ball of each

pair of rubber clogs

2 buttons, maximum $\frac{4}{5}$" (about 20 mm) in diameter, with holes big enough to pass Florida yarn through

1.5–3 mm crochet hook (the smallest size you can comfortably use)

tracing paper

piece of cardboard

tape measure

erasable pen or chalk (capable of marking on rubber)

X-ACTO knife or small, very sharp scissors (such as manicure scissors)

leather punch with settings from 2 to 4.5 mm (see page 169)

sewing needle (size that fits your buttons)

GAUGE

It honestly doesn't matter.

Overview

First you have to make the holes in your clogs that you'll stitch through later. That means measuring, hole punching, and popping out rubber rounds. Then you'll crochet around the big hole in the center, crochet on the flower, and sew the button onto the center of the flower.

Directions

Before you start, know that making these shoes is a lot like your first kindergarten project: it's the easiest thing in the world to make, but it seems awkward and frustrating, and you'll probably throw a few tantrums until you get used to working with the tools. Take your kindergarten teacher's (and my) advice: stay calm, go slowly, and think as you work. I make about 10 pairs a day, and even that's not enough for my customers, so trust me, they are totally worth the patience.

Prepare Clogs

As you work on the holes in your clogs, use the photo on page 161, "Prepared Clogs," as your guide.

Big Center Hole

1. Trace shape shown here onto your tracing paper, transfer it onto cardboard, and cut out the stencil.

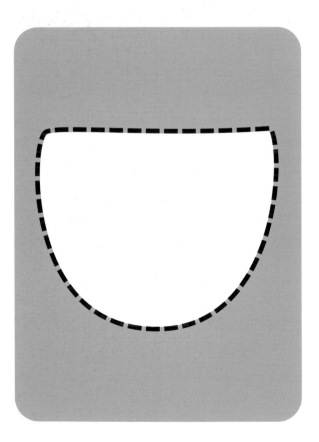

2. Before you put stencil on shoe, mark some measurements on clog itself with erasable pen. Put your foot in shoe, and mark where your toes begin (where they meet your foot, not their tips). If you want your toes to show a little bit, mark end of portion you want to show. Measure 1" from ankle edge of shoe's top, and mark it as well.

3. Now place stencil between these 2 lines (trim it a little if necessary), and trace it with erasable pen.

4. Cut out this large hole with X-ACTO knife or scissors. (Save the piece you cut out. You'll use it later.)

A word to the wise: If you don't have a long history of (successful) experience with X-ACTO knives, use the manicure scissors instead. If you are working with the knife, place something hard inside the shoe to catch and stop the knife. And for God's sake, be careful.

Little Center Holes

Now you need to measure, mark, and punch out little holes around the big hole, so that you have something to insert your hook through.

1. Marking with erasable pen as you go, space little holes 1/5" (about 5 mm) from edge of large hole, with about 1/4" between the dots. It's OK if your 1st and last dots aren't perfectly spaced, but be absolutely sure to get 1 dot at each top corner, or your corner crocheting will look positively awful.

Prepared Clogs

2. Set your hole punch to 3 mm, and punch away.

3. Use your crochet hook to pop those little round suckers out of holes, but, before you do, lock up anything and anyone that eats off the floor until you can take a broom to it.

Flower Holes

Find that piece of rubber you cut out of the center, and put it next to the photo above.

1. Use your pen to copy 1 stemless flower and 1 flower with stem onto the rubber.

Crocheting the Flower Foundation

2. Use 3 mm setting on leather punch to knock out flower center, then set punch to 4.5 mm for petals. Make holes as close to one another as you can without overlapping them. (Don't worry about the pen markings; they'll wipe off later.)

3. For stem, use 3 mm setting for 6 holes closest to flower head and 2.5 mm setting for 7 holes at end.

4. Use 2.5 mm setting for leaf as well, but punch stem-end hole 1st, then 2 side holes closest to it (so that you're sure they're aligned with each other), then 2 side holes toward tip (ditto), then hole at tip of leaf. Try to make sure the 1st 2 side holes are wider apart than the 2nd pair. (Look closely at the photo and you'll see what I mean.)

Now that you've practiced, you can use the punched piece as a stencil on your precious clog—if you did a

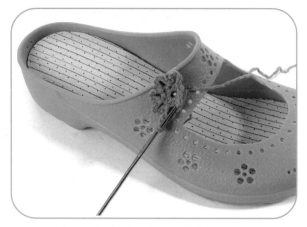

Crocheting Flower Petals

Sewing on the Button

good job on it, that is. Follow the same instructions for marking and punching the holes (just dot through the holes you made in the practice piece), looking at the design in the photo on page 161.

Don't skip the practice. You've been warned.

Crochet Flower

The easiest way to do this is to measure out 16' of **B** and cut it; then work just with that. Build the flower onto the 2nd set of flower holes from the outside edge of the clog—using the center set makes the clog look too schoolgirly, and using the outside set makes the flower scrape against walls, furniture, and whatever else you rub up against.

1. Hold yarn inside shoe, and insert your hook from outside to inside through a petal hole; yo, and pull yarn through to outside. Insert hook in next petal hole, and sl st 1; sl st 1 through each petal hole, then sl st through 1st hole again (see photo on page 161, "Crocheting the Flower Foundation")—you should have a total of 5 sl sts. Pull *all* the yarn through (yes, all 16' of it) to the outside of the shoe. From now on you'll work with everything on the outside.

2. Insert hook under 1st sl st you made, pull yarn under st, and ch 1; insert hook under same sl st again, and sc 1. Now sc 2 under all rem sl sts—9 sc total + 1 ch. Sl st 1 through 1st sc at beg.

3. *Ch 5, and insert hook under next sc to left; rep from * all around flower (see photo above left)—9x total. Sl st 1 under 1st sc in prev rnd.

4. Insert hook inside 1st petal, and sc 5 around the petal's edge (not in the ch sts themselves), then sl

Crocheting Around the Big Hole

st 1 in exactly the same hole on prev row in which you fastened down the ch sts; rep for all 9 petals. Sl st 1 through same 1st sc as in steps 2 and 3.

5. Pull all yarn through to inside, and thread it on sewing needle. Sew button onto flower (see photo on page 162, "Sewing on the Button"), not onto shoe itself. Pull rem yarn through a flower hole to inside of shoe. Tie beg and ending tails tog, and hide them in flower sts on underside of shoe top; stretch shoe a bit to settle tails in place, and cut excess yarn.

Crochet around Big Hole

Set the shoe on a table, and work with it always flat, turning it as necessary to crochet comfortably. For now, set the left shoe so that the toe is pointing left and the heel right, and begin crocheting in the 1st little hole on the side (not in the corner!) closest to you. (In this case, that's the outer side of the shoe. When you get to the right shoe, you want to point it the same way and begin crocheting in the same spot relative to you, which will be the instep of the right shoe.)

1. Holding **A** inside shoe, insert your hook from outside to inside, yo, pull yarn through to outside of shoe, and ch 1.

2. Insert hook into next hole to left, and sc 1; sc 1 in each little hole all around big hole in clog (see photo left).

3. At end, sl st 1 through 1st sc, cut yarn, pull through to inside of shoe, and hide tail by pulling it through at least 3 of the Vs on underside of shoe top. Stretch side of shoe a little to settle tail into place; then cut off excess.

Now *that* is one awesome clog. But you need two!

His Clogs

I call these "his clogs," but in fact
they're a unisex design that anyone
can wear in winter. The problem with rubber clogs in winter is the
gaping hole they leave for your foot, so I just closed that up with a
built-on sock. My clogs are just as suitable for any year-round out-
door activity as your favorite sneakers, only they're waterproof, too.

Overview

First you measure, mark and punch the holes. Then you stitch a foundation row around, and crochet through it to build up stitches with which to crochet the sock. Finally, you weave in a leather tie. That's all there is to it.

Directions

Prepare Clogs

Before you start crocheting, you need to measure and mark where to put all the holes that you're going to crochet through, and then punch out the holes. The holes should be about ²/₅" (about 10 mm) from the edge of the shoe opening, with about ¹/₄" between the dots that mark each hole. Now take this step by step:

1. As you measure, use erasable pen (really, use it) to make dots where you want to punch the holes. Don't start from front of shoe: just in case your 1st and last holes aren't perfectly spaced, you don't want the whole world to see it. Start from either inner side or back of shoe.

2. Set hole punch to 3 mm, and punch holes.

3. Use crochet hook to pop little rounds out of holes. (Lock up your dogs and toddlers until you sweep these up.)

Here are a couple more guidelines before you begin crocheting:

Set the shoe (either one) on a table with the toe pointing right, and keep it flat as you work, turning it to work comfortably. Don't start crocheting at the front of the shoe, because then you'll have to do all your cutting, tying, and hiding from there, which is hard.

You'll be using a very small hook with some very fat yarn (the Boston yarn), because you can't use a bigger hook with the Regia yarn, which is thinner. You're going to have to pass the fat Boston yarn through the tiny Regia yarn, though, so be sure to make your stitches loose.

Crochet Sock

Foundation

Don't make these stitches too tight!

1. With **A** hanging outside, work from inside of shoe as you insert hook through a hole in side of shoe farthest from you (don't worry: it's supposed to be different for right and left), yo, pull yarn through to inside of clog, and sl st 1. (If you're confused, check out the photo, "Crocheting the Foundation" for the Tyler Bucket Bag pattern on page 135, which starts this way.)

2. Sl st 1 in each foll hole; at end of rnd, insert hook again in 1st hole, and sl st 1.

3. Cut yarn, and pull tail through to inside of shoe.

Round 1

Pull beg tail through to inside through next hole to left or right of it (otherwise you'll just undo it). Knot 2 tails tog.

From now on you'll work with the yarn hanging inside the shoe. Continue to work your crocheting on the inside as well.

Rnd 1

1. Insert hook from above under 1 of sl sts in side of shoe closest to you, pull **B** up under st, and ch 3.

2. *Insert hook under next sl st of prev rnd, and dc 1; rep from * all around shoe (see photo above); then sl st 1 through 3rd ch at beg of rnd.

Rnd 2

1. Drop **B** (but don't cut it), and join **A** by pulling it through st left on your hook; ch 2.

Round 3

Finished Sock

2. *Insert hook in next st of prev rnd, and hdc 1; rep from * all around; then sl st 1 through 2nd ch at beg of rnd.

Rnd 3

1. Drop **A** (but don't cut it), pick up **B**, pull it through st left on your hook, and ch 3.

2. *Insert your hook under, *not in*, next hdc of prev rnd, including going under its yo yarn (see photo above), and dc 1; rep from * to end of rnd; sl st 1 through 3rd ch at beg of rnd.

Rnd 4: Windows

1. Pick up **A**, and ch 3 (2 for height, 1 for width).

2. *Insert hook in next st of prev rnd, hdc 1, and ch 1; rep from * to end of rnd; then sl st 1 through 2nd ch at beg of rnd.

3. Cut **B**, and pull it through to inside.

Rnd 5 Cont with **A**, ch 1, then sc 1 under ch betw each hdc on prev rnd; sl st 1 through ch at beg of rnd, and FO.

If you still have any yarn hanging outside shoe, pull it through to inside now. Tie all knots you need, and hide tails.

Now I'll wait while you make the other clog.

Weave In Leather Ties

Quick and simple: use your crochet hook to pull straps through last hdc round. Leave beg tail on outside, and start on outer side of shoe (I doubt he wants to tie the sock from the inside of it or to sport a big sissy bow in front). As you weave leather through crocheting, skip every other hole (see photo above); otherwise it will look too frilly when he ties it.

Tools You'll Need

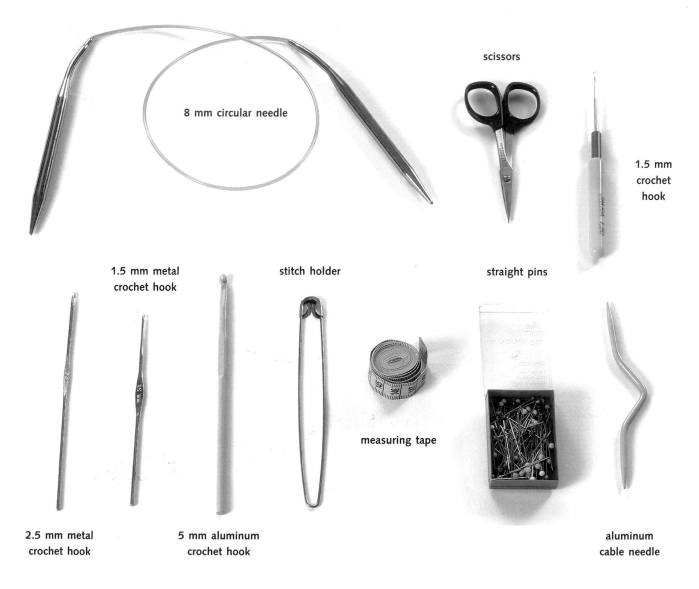

8 mm circular needle

scissors

1.5 mm crochet hook

1.5 mm metal crochet hook

stitch holder

straight pins

2.5 mm metal crochet hook

5 mm aluminum crochet hook

measuring tape

aluminum cable needle

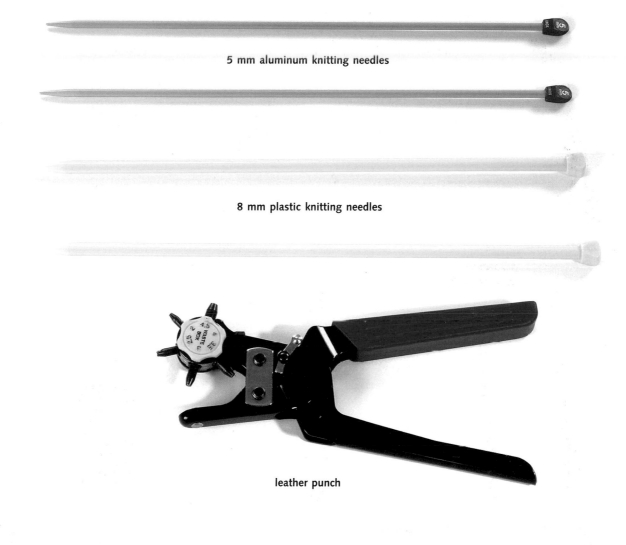

5 mm aluminum knitting needles

8 mm plastic knitting needles

leather punch

Resources for Ordering European Yarns Online

www.theknitter.com

www.royalyarns.com

www.diamondyarn.com
   (my personal favorite)

www.yarnmarket.com

www.knitntyme.com

www.onefineyarn.com

www.fibershop.com

www.beehivewool.com

Table of Abbreviations

approx = approximately

beg = begin(ning) (began)

betw = between

BO = bind off [knit]

CC = contrasting color (yarn in a garment)

ch = chain (stitch)

CO = cast on

cont = continue(d) (s) (ing)

dc = double crochet

dec = decrease(d) (ing) (s)

dtr = double treble crochet

FO = fasten off [crochet]

foll = follow(ing)

hdc = half double crochet

inc = increase(d) (ing) (s)

k = knit

L = large (size of garment)

M = medium (size of garment)

MC = main color (yarn in a pattern)

mm = millimeters

oz = ounces

p = purl

patt = pattern

prev = previous

quintr = double treble treble crochet (sort of)

rem = remain(ing) (s)

rep = repeat(ed) (ing) (s)

rib = rib(bing)

rnd(s) = round(s)

RS = right side

S = small (size of garment)

sc = single crochet (stitch)

skp = slip, knit, pass slipped stitch over

sl st = slip stitch

st(s) = stitch(es)

St st = stockinette stitch

tog = together

tr = treble crochet

trtr = treble treble crochet

WS = wrong side

x = times

XL = extra large (size of garment)

yds = yards

yo = yarn over

METRIC CONVERSION CHART

Inches	Millimeters
1/8	3.2
1/4	6.4
3/8	9.5
1/2	12.7
5/8	15.9
3/4	19.1
7/8	22.2
1	25.4
2	50.8
3	76.2
4	101.6
5	127.0
6	152.4
7	177.8
8	203.2
9	228.6
10	25.4
11	279.4
12	304.8

About the Author

Lena Maikon learned to knit at the age of five in her hometown of Novosibirsk, Russia. She didn't pick up a needle again until she turned thirty, when she realized her talent for knitting could save her from a frustrating career as a math teacher. Encouraged by the thought that she could make all those expensive store-bought knits herself, she began applying her mathematical mind to the counting of stitches. Proud of her Russian heritage, Lena developed the clothing label "Leninka." Her handmade knits are sought after in the fashionable boutiques of New York's Soho and in her adopted city of Tel Aviv, Israel, where her chic garments dress windows along trendy boulevards downtown.

Index